Bride of Ice: New Sele~~ ~

MARINA TSVETAEVA was born in Mo,
a professor of art history at the Universit
who died of TB when Tsvetaeva was f(
Tsvetaeva's first poems, *Evening Album*, w(～ ⅃⁊⒣0. In
1912 Tsvetaeva married Sergei Efron,   ..ı1om she had two
daughters, Alya and Irina. During the Civil War Efron fought in the
White Army while Tsvetaeva and the children endured the Moscow
famine. Irina died of starvation in 1920. In 1922 the Civil War ended
with Bolshevik victory and Tsvetaeva joined Efron in exile in Prague. It
was here that she wrote some of her greatest poetry. In 1924
Tsvetaeva's son Georgy was born. The family moved to Paris in 1925.
Tsvetaeva became isolated from Russian literary émigrés and,
increasingly, from Efron and Alya, whose allegiances moved towards
Communism. Both returned to Russia in 1937, Alya freely and Efron
to avoid arrest for his involvement in the murder of a defector.
Tsvetaeva followed him to Russia with Georgy in 1939, unaware of Stalin's
Terror. Alya was arrested and sentenced to fifteen years in prison.
Efron was shot in 1941. In the same year, following the German
invasion, Tsvetaeva and Georgy left Moscow for Yelabuga in the Tartar
Republic. Tsvetaeva hanged herself there on 31 August 1941.

ELAINE FEINSTEIN was educated at Newnham College, Cambridge.
She has worked as a university lecturer, a subeditor, and a freelance
journalist. Since 1980, when she was made a Fellow of the Royal
Society of Literature, she has lived as a full-time writer. In 1990,
she received a Cholmondeley Award for Poetry, and was given an
Honorary D.Litt from the University of Leicester. Her versions of the
poems of Marina Tsvetaeva – for which she received three translation
awards from the Arts Council –were first published in 1971. She has
written fourteen novels, many radio plays, television dramas, and five
biographies, including *A Captive Lion: the Life of Marina Tsvetaeva*
(1987) and *Pushkin* (1998). *Anna of all the Russias: The Life of Anna
Akhmatova* was published in 2005. Elaine Feinstein's *Collected Poems
and Translations* (2002) was a Poetry Book Society Special Comm-
endation. Her evocation of Stalin's Russia, *The Russian Jerusalem*, was
published by Carcanet Press in 2008. She served on the Council of the
Royal Society of Literature, of which she was a Fellow, as a judge for
most of the current literary prizes, and as Chair of the Judges for the
T.S.Eliot Award. She received a Civil List Pension in 2010. She died in
September 2019.

Also by Elaine Feinstein from Carcanet Press

Poetry
Daylight
Gold
Selected Poems
Collected Poems and Translations
Talking to the Dead

Fiction
The Russian Jerusalem

As editor
After Pushkin

Russian poetry from Carcanet Press

Alexander Blok, *Selected Poems*, trans. Jon Stallworthy and Peter France
Joseph Brodsky, *Collected Poems in English*, trans. Anthony Hecht,
Howard Moss, Derek Walcott, Richard Wilbur et al.
After Pushkin, ed. Elaine Feinstein
An Anthology of Contemporary Russian Women Poets ed. Valentina
Polukhina and Daniel Weissbort
What I Own: Versions of Holderlin and Mandelshtam by John Riley
and Tim Longville

MARINA TSVETAEVA

Bride of Ice: New Selected Poems

Translated with an introduction by
Elaine Feinstein

from literal versions by
Daisy Cockburn, Valentina Coe, Bernard Comrie,
Simon Franklin, Jana Howlett, Angela Livingstone,
Cathy Porter, Tatiana Retivov, Maxwell Shorter
and Vera Traill

CARCANET CLASSICS

First published as *Selected Poems* in 1971 by Oxford University Press
Revised, enlarged and reissued 1981, 1986, 1993, 1999, 2009
This revised and enlarged sixth edition published in 2023 by
Carcanet Press Limited
Alliance House
Cross Street
Manchester M2 7AQ

Selection, translations and notes copyright © Elaine Feinstein 1971, 1981,
1986, 1993, 1999, 2009, 2023
Introduction and bibliography copyright © Elaine Feinstein 2009

The right of Elaine Feinstein to be identified as the editor and translator
of this work has been asserted by her in accordance with the
Copyright, Designs and Patents Act of 1988
All rights reserved

A CIP catalogue record for this book is available from the British Library
ISBN 978 1 80017 227 2

The publisher acknowledges financial assistance from Arts Council England

Typeset by XL Publishing Services, Tiverton
Printed and bound in England by SRP Ltd, Exeter

Contents

List of Collaborators

Literal versions of the poems were provided by the following:

Valentina Coe
POEM OF THE MOUNTAIN

Daisy Cockburn
Verse
Your narrow, foreign shape

Bernard Comrie
Yesterday he still looked in my eyes

Simon Franklin
God help us   Smoke!
Ophelia: In Defence of the Queen
from WIRES: Lyric 1
Sahara
Appointment
Rails
You loved me
To Boris Pasternak
from THE RATCATCHER: from Chapter 1 and from Chapter 2
Desk
Bus

Jana Howlett
from SWANS' ENCAMPMENT

Angela Livingstone
I know the truth
What is this gypsy passion for separation
We shall not escape Hell
We are keeping an eye on the girls
No one has taken anything away
You throw back your head

Introduction

The poetry of Marina Tsvetaeva drew me initially[1] through the intensity of her emotions, and the honesty with which she exposed them. In this, she has remained an enduring and exacting mentor. Her themes, too, seemed immediately relevant: her desperate need for love, and the tension between poetry and domestic responsibilities. Over the years I celebrated her dedication to poetry, while hardly touching on the ruthlessness which underpinned her stamina, still less the inner vulnerabilities that lay beneath her wilfulness. In 2008 I invented her as a Virgil to lead me around Stalin's Hell in *The Russian Jerusalem*. In doing so, I became uneasily aware of elements in her complex personality given greater prominence in other biographies. This new selection of her poems contains several sequences which suggest the sources of her own inspiration, and her longing for intimacy with poets of equal genius.

Marina Ivanovna Tsvetaeva (1892–1941) was the daughter of a Professor of Fine Arts at Moscow University, and grew up in material comfort. Her mother, Maria, was by far the most powerful presence in the household; a gifted woman, of bitter intensity, she had renounced her first love to marry a widower much older than herself. Her considerable musical talents were frustrated, and she turned all her energies towards educating Marina, her precocious elder daughter. Insistence on hours of music practice and a stern refusal of any words of praise made Marina's childhood unusually austere.

When Marina was fourteen, her mother died of tuberculosis, expressing a passionate indifference to the world she was leaving: 'I only regret music and the sun.' After her death, Marina abandoned the study of music and began to develop her passion for literature. 'After a mother like that,' she reflected, 'I had only one alternative: to become a poet.'[2]

Her mother remained in her dreams, sometimes as a longed-for, benevolent figure. In one dream, however, Tsvetaeva meets a bent old woman who whispers surprisingly: 'A mean little thing she was, a clinging one, believe me, sweetheart.' This is the witchy crone of

Russian folklore, and we meet her again in Tsvetaeva's cruel fairy tale 'On a Red Horse'.

By the age of eighteen, Tsvetaeva had acquired sufficient reputation as a poet to be welcome as a house guest at the Crimean dacha of Maximilian Voloshin. There she met her future husband, Sergei Efron, the half-Jewish orphan of an earlier generation of revolutionaries. At seventeen, he was shy, with huge grey eyes, overwhelmed by Tsvetaeva's poetic genius. They fell instantly in love, and his was the most loyal affection Tsvetaeva was ever to find. They were married in January 1912. For two years after their marriage, they were irresponsibly happy together. Seryozha, as he was usually known, was an aspirant writer and a charming actor. Most people who knew Efron liked him, but some thought him too much under the influence of his wife. He was certainly weak physically – he suffered from TB all his life – but Irma Kudrova, recently allowed access to files of his 1940 NKVD interrogations,[3] has uncovered a man of unusual courage and integrity.

When war came in August 1914, Seryozha was eager to enlist, and was sent initially to the front line as a male nurse in an ambulance train. Soon afterwards, Tsvetaeva fell in love with Sofia Parnok, a talented poet from a middle-class Jewish family in the Black Sea port of Taganrog. Tsvetaeva had been wildly but innocently attracted to beautiful young girls in her early adolescence, but Parnok was an open lesbian. She was not exactly beautiful, but she possessed a sexual assurance which had never been the main bond in Tsvetaeva's affection for Seryozha.

Tsvetaeva was well provided for since her father's death in 1913, and for fifteen months she threw herself into her passion for Parnok, with little thought for her husband and two-year-old child. She and Parnok travelled brazenly over the wilds of Russia together and even visited Voloshin's dacha. The lyrics for Parnok are both more sensual, and less tormented, than other love poetry written by Tsvetaeva. Sergei had a brief love affair of his own.

In Parnok's poems for Tsvetaeva, she describes her as an 'awkward little girl', but her claim to have been the first to give Tsvetaeva intense sexual pleasure may have been no more than a boast. In any case, as the affair came to an end, it soon became clear that it was to Seryozha that Tsvetaeva felt the strongest bond. When the Revolution came, she was in hospital giving birth to their second child. Separated from him in the confusion at the start of the Civil War, she wrote in her diary: 'If God performs this miracle and leaves you alive, I will follow you like a dog.'

Through the Moscow famine, Tsvetaeva and her two children lived in Boris and Gleb Lane, in unheated rooms, sometimes without light. She and Efron were to be separated for five years. In those years, she and her elder daughter, Ariadne, were almost like sisters. Alya, as she was usually called was as precociously observant a child as Tsvetaeva had been herself. This is how she writes of Tsvetaeva:

> My mother is not at all like a mother. Mothers always think their own children are wonderful, and other children too, but Marina doesn't like little children... She is always hurrying somewhere. She has a great soul. A kind voice. A quick walk. She has green eyes, a hooked nose and red lips... Marina's hands are all covered with rings... she doesn't like people bothering her with stupid questions...[4]

The family fared badly in the Moscow famine. Marina was unskilled at bartering trinkets for food, and she and Alya often lived on potatoes boiled in a samovar. They sometimes went out on a sledge together in the freezing cold to exchange bottle tops for a few kopeks, often leaving the younger child, Irina, strapped against a table leg to prevent her coming to harm. When starvation looked imminent in the winter of 1919-20, Tsvetaeva put both children into the Kuntsevo orphanage, which was thought to be supplied by American food aid. When she arrived on her first visit, Alya was running a high temperature and Tsvetaeva, frightened, took her home to nurse her. Alya pulled through but Irina died of starvation in the orphanage in February 1920. Tsvetaeva was unable to make herself go to the funeral. She blamed Seryozha's sisters, probably unfairly, for refusing to help her, claiming they had behaved 'like animals'. She told all her friends to write to Seryozha that the child had died of pneumonia rather than hunger. There was much gossip about her own neglect of the child. Certainly, she was never as close to Irina as to Alya.

The following year was taken up by a new infatuation – Yevgeny Lann, a poet friend of her sister Asya – a humiliating rejection by him, and anxiety about Seryozha as the defeat of the White Army loomed closer. In January 1921, Tsvetaeva wrote a poem of pitiless inquiry into the nature of her own inspiration: 'On a Red Horse'. The tone resembles that of her other folkloric poems of the period such as 'The Tsar Maiden' (1920) and 'The Swain' (1922) but the story of 'On a Red Horse' is not taken from one of Alexander Afansyev's volumes of Russian fairy tales; it is her own invention. A handsome rider of implacable cruelty demands that all her other loves be sacrificed for him. These dream-like sacrifices do not secure his kindness, however, and an old woman she encounters reveals the bleak truth: '*Your Angel doesn't love you!*' Released from the hope of winning his affection, she plunges into battle as a male figure. A phrase from the resolution of this poem gives this book its title:

And he whispers *I wanted this.*
It is for this I chose you,
you are my passion, my sister,
mine till the end of time

my bride of ice – in armour –
Mine. Will you stay with me…[5]

In 1922, the Civil War ended in victory for the Bolsheviks. Ilya Ehrenburg, who was always in touch with what was happening to his friends, learned that Seryozha had made his escape to Prague, where he had been offered a student grant to study at the university. Ehrenburg brought Tsvetaeva the news and, without hesitation, she and Alya prepared to set off into exile to join him – though it has to be said that Tsvetaeva found Berlin almost irresistibly exciting along the way. When the family was reunited, she was shocked to find how little Seryozha had changed from the boyish young man she remembered. She herself had been shattered by her experience and was prematurely grey at thirty. In Prague, Seryozha was given a room in a student hostel, while Tsvetaeva and Alya lived in the village of Horni Mokropsky.

At first, Tsvetaeva was welcomed in Prague as a major literary figure, but her more conventional compatriots soon turned away from her. She failed, as Nina Berberova makes clear in her autobiography *The Italics Are Mine*,[6] to show the domestic graces that make poverty bearable. Men of comparable genius usually find women to take care of them. Anna Akhmatova, Tsvetaeva's only equal as a Russian woman poet, always found friends to look after her, even in old age. Tsvetaeva was less fortunate and she resented the burden of the daily round. Nevertheless, it was in Prague that she had her short, fierce affair with Konstantin Rodzevich, which drew from her some of her greatest poetry: 'Poem of the End', 'Poem of the Mountain' and 'An Attempt at Jealousy'. Rodzevich ended the affair, and went on to marry an 'ordinary' woman with a private income.

When I met Rodzevich in the 1970s, while writing my biography of Tsvetaeva, he was a handsome, well-dressed man in late middle-age. His wife was so jealous of him that he would only agree to meet me when he was sure she would be out. He talked of his love for Tsvetaeva as *un grand amour* and showed me a portrait he had painted of her which he kept in a locked drawer. Why then had he ended their affair? He attributed this to the great affection he felt for Seryozha. I was sceptical, but I was already suspicious of him. He had fought in the Red Army in the Civil War, but told the émigrés in Prague that he had been part of the White Army, a well-judged subterfuge which did not suggest he was particularly trustworthy.

He had two other secrets, however, which I have only recently discovered. I knew he was an enthusiastic member of the Eurasian movement, along with Seryozha, who drew a salary from it, and my old Cambridge friend Vera Traill's husband Peter Suvchinsky. I knew, too, that this became a front organisation for the NKVD. What I had not guessed was that Rodzevich was himself working as a Soviet agent. Nor did I guess that he was Vera Traill's lover. That last is evident in an intimate and long-running exchange of letters discussed in Irma Kudrova's *Death of a Poet* and throws new light on Vera's irritable dismissal of Tsvetaeva's womanliness, even as she praised her genius as a poet.

About one thing Rodzevich was accurate enough. The distress of Tsvetaeva's affair drove Seryozha to the point of leaving her. When he suggested separation to Tsvetaeva, however, she was distraught. 'For two weeks she was in a state of madness... finally she informed me that she was unable to leave me since she was unable to enjoy a moment's peace.'[7]

Tsvetaeva has often been accused of preferring to make her closest relationships at a distance, usually inventing the qualities of their recipients. Indeed, she was locked in an epistolary romance with a young Berlin critic whom she had never met at the very moment she entered her affair with Rodzevich. Her important relationship with Boris Pasternak is another matter. For one thing, it was initiated by him and his enthusiasm was equal to hers.

She and Pasternak had only known one another slightly in Moscow; though he was one of the poets she most admired. Pasternak wrote to her after reading a copy of Tsvetaeva's early poems, overwhelmed by her lyric genius. His words – 'You are not a child, my dear, golden, incomparable poet,' [8] – restored her sense of her own worth. Their correspondence continued with mounting warmth, as poems and plans for poems were exchanged. She had found a twin soul. Soon, he was suggesting that she join him in Berlin where he was visiting his parents. She failed to arrange the correct papers in time, and he returned to Russia without meeting her, though they continued to plan for it. In 1931, when she heard that Pasternak had separated from his wife, she seems to have experienced a kind of panic. She wrote to her friend Raisa Lomonsova: 'For eight years Boris and I had a secret agreement: to keep on until we can be together. But the *catastrophe* of a meeting kept being postponed.' It seems likely that she was afraid of being rejected as a woman. Her cycle of lyrics, 'Wires', is an extraordinary example of the poems he drew from her. Two of these appeared in my earlier selection, but both are amended here, and the other eight are now included.

The only other poet to whom Tsvetaeva wrote with comparable excitement was Rainer Maria Rilke, in 1926. The correspondence came about after Leonid Pasternak, Boris's painter father, received a letter from Rilke, whose portrait he had made when the German poet visited Moscow. In his letter, Rilke praised the poems of Leonid's son, which he was able to read in a French translation in a journal edited by Paul Valéry. Pasternak was overwhelmed with joy to hear as much, and was eager to include Tsvetaeva in the exchange. She took up the opportunity enthusiastically, perhaps a little too eagerly for Rilke, who was lying mortally ill in a sanatorium. She was unhappy to discover that he was unable to read her poems in Russian and, after a few exchanges, he fell silent, which she took as rejection. There is a sad postcard from Bellevue dated 7 November 1926 on which Tsvetaeva writes simply:

Dear Rainer,
This is where I live.
Do you still love me?
Marina[9]

The elegy she wrote for his death at the end of 1926 has been analysed with great eloquence in an essay of Joseph Brodsky, 'Footnote to a Poem' [10] He praises the amazing energy miraculously sustaining a sequence which has the nerve, as he puts it, to open on 'High C'. In it, we are transported from the ordinary chat of the literary world to look back on the earth as if from a theatre box far out in the universe.

Do you ever – think about me, I wonder?
What do you feel now, what is it like up there?
How was your first sight of the Universe,
a last vision of the whole planet –
which must include this poet remaining in it,
not yet ashes, still a spirit in a body –
seen from however many miles stretch
from Creation to eternity, far above
the Mediterranean in its crystal saucer –
where else would you look, leaning out
with your elbows on the edge of your box seat
if not on this poet, with her many griefs…[11]

Seryozha and Marina had one more child, a son, Georgy, before they moved to Paris. For a time, Seryozha found work as a film extra, but he was often ill, and Tsvetaeva tried to sustain their finances by writing articles for the Russian-language press and accepting charitable handouts from richer friends. She gave the occasional reading, for which she had to beg a simple washable dress from her Czech friend Anna Teskovà. As she wrote in a letter to Teskova: 'We are devoured by coal, gas, the milkman, the baker… the only meat we eat is horsemeat.'[12]

Seryozha moved from support of the Eurasian Movement to working directly for the Union of Repatriation of Russians abroad.

From this organization, he drew a small salary. Tsvetaeva inquired very little into the nature of this work. Her own isolation among White émigrés grew, and not only because of her refusal to sign a letter condemning Mayakovsky's talents as a poet after his suicide. 'In Paris,' she wrote to her Czech friend Anna Teskova, 'with rare personal exceptions, everyone hates me; they write all sorts of nasty things about me, leave me out in all sorts of ways, and so on.'[13] Sadly, she came to feel equally isolated in her own home. Alya, once so close, had begun to find it easier to relate to her father. Both Seryozha and Alya moved towards the ideals of socialism as the 1930s went on. As soon as Alya was given a passport by the Soviet regime, she made her own way back to Russia. It was never going to be easy for Seryozha to do the same. The Soviet authorities had not forgotten that he once fought for the White Army and demanded some evidence of a change of heart; hence, although he was an unlikely hit-man, Seryozha's involvement in the murder of the defector Ignace Reiss in September 1937. Tsvetaeva guessed nothing of his activities until the Soviet regime arranged for his passage back to Russia to prevent his arrest. Even when the French police interrogated her, she found it impossible to believe that Seryozha was guilty of such treachery.

With his departure, she no longer had any source of income. No émigré journal would publish her. Friends who had once supported her, turned their backs. She hesitated, nevertheless, even though her teenage son Georgy was eager to return to Russia. For a time she toyed with living once again in Prague. The German invasion made that impossible. By 1939, she and Georgy had little choice but to follow Efron back to Russia, as she had once followed him into exile; ' like a dog', as she noted in the journal she wrote aboard the *Maria Ulyanova* on 12 June 1939, echoing her earlier promise.

Nobody had warned her about Stalin's Terror, not even Pasternak, who had met her briefly in Paris in 1935 during a Peace Conference – a 'non-meeting' she called it. In any case, that great weariness which she evoked in her poem 'Bus' already consumed her. She found Efron had been given a small house in Bolshevo, a little way outside Moscow. Other news was bewildering. Both her sister Asya and her nephew had been arrested. Her old friend Prince Mirsky, a dedicated Communist and brilliant literary critic, had also been imprisoned. Osip Mandelstam was dead.

Tsvetaeva felt lonely in Bolshevo even while her own surviving family were still with her. Other members of the household were members of the group of Soviet agents Seryozha had recruited in France. Her son, a good-looking young man, enjoyed teenage flirtations. Tsvetaeva had neither time nor energy to write more than scraps. 'Dishwater and tears', she jotted in a notebook. The year of the Nazi–Soviet pact was a crisis. Worse was to follow. First Alya was arrested, and interrogated brutally; as a result she implicated Seryozha as a French spy. Alya was sentenced to fifteen years in the Gulag in spite of her 'confession'. Then Seryozha himself was arrested.

When Tsvetaeva visited Moscow, she found old friends were afraid to meet her, as a relation of convicted criminals. Even Ehrenburg was brusque and preoccupied. Pasternak received her without the least intimacy during a party for Georgian friends. Anna Akhmatova, however, agreed to meet her at the flat of Viktor Ardov on the Ordynka, an act of some courage since her own son, Lev, was already held in the Camps. Akhmatova never discussed what was said between them, but in later conversations she remembered reading Tsvetaeva part of 'Poem Without a Hero', noting ironically that Tsvetaeva objected to her use of figures from *commedia dell'arte*. Tsvetaeva read her part of her 'Attempt at a Room', which Akhmatova thought too abstract.

The two women were very different creatures. Tsvetaeva did not perceive herself as a beautiful woman. She once remarked scornfully that, although she would be the most important woman in all her friends' memoirs, she 'had never counted in the masculine present'. After her affair with Rodzevich ended, she wrote poignantly to her young friend Bakhrakh in Berlin: 'To be loved is something of which I have not mastered the art...'[14] Yet Tsvetaeva had her own sense of grandeur. She knew herself to belong among the finest poets of her century. She did not make the mistake of blurring the distinction between serving poetry and serving God, any more than she would ever allow for poetry the utilitarian hope that Art can do civic good. In the closing passage from 'Art in the Light of Conscience' she makes that clear: 'To be a human being is more important, because it is more needed... The doctor and the priest are humanly more important, all the others are socially more important.'[15] Tsvetaeva had written no more than scraps of journal for nearly two years.

When the Germans invaded Russia in 1941, Tsvetaeva evacuated Georgy and herself to Yelabuga in the Tatar Republic, just across the river Kama from Christopol where the Writers' Union was housing key writers. Tsvetaeva was not denied lodging there, but she feared there would be no job for her. Her indecision was obvious to Ludia Chukovskaya, Akhmatova's friend. It may be that she heard then that Seryozha had already been shot in the Lubianka. Whatever the trigger, the depression which gripped her was deepened by Georgy's hostility when she returned to the village hut in Yelabuga. She took her own life there by hanging herself from a nail on 31 August 1941.

★

All translation is difficult; Tsvetaeva is a particularly difficult poet. Her pauses and sudden changes of speed are felt always against the deliberate constraint of the forms she had chosen. Perhaps the exact metres could not be kept, but some sense of her shapeliness, as well as her roughness, had to survive. For this reason I usually followed her stanzaic patterning, though I have frequently indented lines where she does not. This slight shift is one of many designed to dispel any sense of the static solidity which blocks of lines convey to an English eye, and which is not induced by the Russian.

English poetry demands a natural syntax, and in looking for that I observed that some of Tsvetaeva's abruptness had been smoothed out, and the poems had gained a different, more logical scheme of development. There were other problems. Tsvetaeva's punctuation is strongly individual; but to have reproduced it pedantically would often have destroyed the tone of the English version. In my first drafts I experimented with using extra spaces between words, but sometimes restored Tsvetaeva's dash, at least in the early poems; in later poems a space has often seemed closer to the movement of her lines. Dashes that indicated the beginning of direct speech are retained, but for this edition I have made clearer who is speaking in lyrics 5 and 6 of 'Poem of the End'. I frequently left out exclamation marks where their presence seemed to weaken a line that was already loud and vibrant. Furthermore, there were difficulties of diction. Words with echoes of ancient folksongs and the Bible were particularly hard to carry across into English.

I am not sure how far a discussion of methods of translation attracts much useful reflection. Yet some word seems necessary, especially since I have worked with different linguists. Some of the poems, such as 'Poem of the End', as Angela Livingstone describes in her detailed Note on Working Method, p. 164, below, were transliterated into English, as well as written out in word-for-word literal versions, which indicated, by hyphenation, words that represented a single Russian word. Other poems, such as the 'Insomnia' cycle and 'Verses about Moscow', also prepared for me by Angela Livingstone, were first read on to tape in Russian; and then (on the same tape) as literal versions which I wrote out myself and used alongside the printed Russian text. For 'An Attempt at Jealousy' I used the literal prose version at the foot of the page in the *Penguin Book of Russian Verse*. For the 1981 edition, Simon Franklin produced written literal versions very much as Angela Livingstone had done, though without transliterations; and he too gave full indications in his notes of changes of rhythm, musical stress and word-play.

The poems are arranged in order of their original composition, with the new translations fitted into the chronology. Chronological order is particularly important for an understanding of many of the poems.

All my collaborators are listed in full on p. vii, but I should particularly like to acknowledge the work of Tatiana Retivov, once a student of Joseph Brodsky, who made literal versions of all the new lyrics for this edition, alongside the Cyrillic text, and made useful comments. Naturally, all distortions introduced in order to turn these versions into English poems are my responsibility.

Elaine Feinstein
January 2009

Notes

1 *Selected Poems of Marina Tsvetaeva*, trans. Elaine Feinstein (Oxford University Press 1971; paperback enlarged edition, Oxford University Press 1981; third edition re-issued Hutchinson 1986; fourth, further enlarged, edition, with revised introduction, Oxford Poets, Oxford University Press 1993; enlarged fifth edition Carcanet Press 1999).

2 'Mother and Music', in J. Marin King (ed.), *A Captive Spirit: Selected Prose of Marina Tsvetayeva* (Ann Arbor, Ardis 1980), p. 276.

3 Irma Kudrova, *Death of a Poet: The Last Days of Marina Tsvetaeva*, trans. Mary Ann Szporluk (London, Duckworth 2004), pp. 99–114.

4 Elaine Feinstein, *A Captive Lion: The Life of Marina Tsvetayeva* (London, Hutchinson 1987), p. 65.

5 'On a Red Horse', p. 60, below.

6 Nina Berberova, *The Italics are Mine: Memoirs of the Russian Literary Emigration*, trans. Philippe Radley (New York, Harcourt, Brace and World 1969), *passim*.

7 Viktoria Schweitzer, *Tsvetaeva*, trans. Robert Chandler and H.T. Willetts (London, HarperCollins 1992), p. 242.

8 Letter from Boris Pasternak, 13 June 1922, in Elaine Feinstein, *Marina Tsvetaeva* (Lives of Modern Women, Harmondsworth, Penguin 1989), p.102.

9 Yevgeny Pasternak, Yelena Pasternak and Konstantin M. Azadovsky (eds), *Boris Pasternak, Marina Tsvetaeva, Rainer Maria Rilke: Letters, Summer 1926*, trans. Mararet Wettlin and Walter Arndt (London, Jonathan Cape 1986), p. 264.

10 'Footnote to a Poem', in Joseph Brodsky, *Less than One: Selected Essays* (New York, Farrar, Straus, and Giroux 1986), p. 195.

11 'New Year's Greetings', p. 121, below.

12 Feinstein, *A Captive Lion*, p. 186.

13 Feinstein, *A Captive Lion*, p. 146.

14 Feinstein, *A Captive Lion*, ibid.

15 Marina Tsvetaeva, *Art in the Light of Conscience: Eight Essays on Poetry*, trans. Angela Livingstone (London, Bristol Classical 1992).

POEMS

Verse

Written so long ago, I didn't even
    know I was a poet,
my lines fell like spray from a fountain
    or flashes from a rocket,

like imps, they burst into sanctuaries
    filled with sleep and incense,
to speak of youth and dying.
    All my unread pages

lie scattered in dusty bookshops
    where nobody picks them up
to this day. Like expensive wines,
    your time will come, my lines.

May 1913

from *GIRLFRIEND*

1

Are you happy? You never tell me.
  Maybe it's better like this.
You've kissed so many others –
  which makes for sadness.

In you, I see the heroines
  of Shakespeare's tragedies.
You, unhappy lady, were
  never saved by anybody.

You have grown tired of repeating
  the familiar words of love!
An iron ring on a bloodless hand
  is more expressive,

I love you – like a storm burst
  overhead – I must confess it;
all the more fiercely because you burn
  and bite, and most of all

because our secret lives take
  very different paths:
seduction and dark fate
  are your inspiration.

To you, my aquiline demon,
  I apologise. In a flash –
as if over a coffin – I realise
  it was always too late to save you!

Even as I tremble – it may be
  I am dreaming – there
remains one enchanting irony:
  for *you* – are not *he*.

16 October 1914

4

2

Beneath this caressing, plush blanket
   I call up yesterday's dream.
What was it? Whose was the victory?
   Who was defeated?

As I think it over again and again
   I keep trying to find
the words for what happened:
   Was it love?

Who was the hunter? Who the prey?
   The roles reverse.
What does the Siberian tiger
   understand as he purrs?

Who in our duel of wills
   was left holding a bauble?
Was it your heart – or mine
   flew off at a gallop?

And, after all, what did happen?
   Something desired – or regretted?
I can't decide if I won
   or if I was conquered,

                23 October 1914

3

Today it thawed, today
   I stood by the window
soberly, with my lungs free,
   almost satisfied.

I don't know why – maybe,
   my soul is tired –
I had no wish to touch
   my mutinous pencil.

Instead I stood in a mist
   neither good nor wicked,
with my finger quietly prodding
   the window pane.

My soul felt no better and no worse
   than that passer-by over there
or those puddles of mother-of-pearl
   splattered by the sky,

the bird flying above
   or a dog running;
even a beggar's song does not
   move me to tears.

Sweetly and cleverly, forgetfulness
   has already taken over –
and by today another huge emotion
   has melted in my soul.

24 October 1914

4

You were too lazy to dress yourself,
   or get up from the armchair.
– When I go towards you, the day
   is joyful with my happiness.

You were troubled about leaving
   so late at night in the cold.
– Any hour when I approach you
   is healthy with my joy.

You mean no harm by any of this,
    unchangeably innocent,
— I am your youth, which already
    begins to pass you by.

25 October 1914

5

About eight this evening, a sleigh
    rushed past me, recklessly,
along Bolshaya Lubyanka
    like a bullet or a snowball.

I heard your tinkling laugh
    in the distance and froze,
staring: your fawn-coloured fur,
    the tall figure at your side...

You are enjoying the pleasures
    of a sleigh with someone else,
a chosen lover, already more
    desired than I was!

— *Oh, je n'en puis plus, j'étouffe,*
    you screamed at me today.
And now, boldly, you cover her
    with the furs inside the sleigh.

The rest of the world is happy.
    The evening glamorous.
Gifts and muffs... and you both rushing
    into the blizzard — fur to fur.

Then a brutal surge of snow
    turns everything white.
I could only follow the two of you
    for a matter of seconds.

I stroke the long hair on my
    coat and feel no anger...
Your little Kay has frozen to death
    O great Snow Queen.

                    26 October 1914

6

Night weeps over coffee grounds
    as it looks to the east.
Its mouth is a tender blossom
    but it has a monstrous flower.

Soon a young, thin moon will take
    the place of scarlet dawn,
and I shall give you many
    combs and rings.

The young moon between the branches
    never guards anyone.
I shall give you ear-rings
    bracelets, and chains!

Your bright eyes sparkle, as if
    from under a heavy mane.
Are your horses jealous – those
    thoroughbreds, so light on their feet?

9

You entered with incomparable panache,
    and I dared not touch your hand.
Already I could feel the pain of longing
    as if you were my very first love.

My heart whispered: *Darling!*
   I forgave you in advance,
without knowing your name, I murmured
   Love me! Please love me!

I looked at the curve of your lips,
   that deliberate arrogance,
those heavy eyebrows – and
   my heart began to thunder.

Your dress was a silky black shell,
   your voice husky as a gypsy;
everything about you sweetly poignant
   – even the fact you are no beauty.

You won't fade over the summer even
   if your flower and stalk are not steely,
for you are meaner and sharper than any
   – from what island do you come,

with that huge fan, and walking stick?
   In every bone, and wicked finger
I make out the gentleness of a woman
   and the audacity of a boy.

How shall I treat these ironies in verse
   or explain to the world
all the qualities I see in you?
   My stranger with Beethoven's brow!

14 January 1915

How can I forget that perfume
  of White Rose and tea,
those figures of Sèvres above
  a blazing fireplace.

There we stood. I was dressed
  in splendid golden silk.
You – in a black knit jacket
  with a winged collar.

As you entered, I remember your face
  was almost colourless;
you stood biting a finger,
  your head slightly tilted.

A helmet of red hair surrounded
  your powerful forehead.
You were neither woman nor boy –
  but stronger than I was.

With no reason to move, I stood up
  and at once people gathered round –
someone even tried, as if in a joke,
  to introduce us.

How calmly you put
  your hand in mine,
and left in my palm a lingering
  splinter of ice.

You took out a cigarette.
  I offered you a light,
afraid of what I might do
  if you looked into my face.

I remember how our glasses clinked
   over a blue vase. *Please*
be my Orestes, I murmured
   – and gave you a flower.

Your grey eyes flashed as you took
   a handkerchief out of your
black suede purse – and slowly
   let it drop to the floor.

28 January 1915

11

Many eyes sparkle under the sun
   and one day is not
like another. Let me tell you this,
   in case I am unfaithful:

whoever I am kissing
   in the hour of love,
whatever vows I make
   in the dark of night

– since I can't live like
   an obedient child
or bloom like a flower without
   looking at anyone else –

I swear by this cross of cypress
   – you know it well –
if you whistle under my window
   all my love will re-awaken.

22 February 1915

12

Moscow's hills are blue, the warm air
   tasting of dust and tar.
I sleep all day or else I laugh
   as if well again after winter.

I go home quietly without regretting
   the poems I haven't written,
the sound of wheels, or roasted almonds
   matter more than a quatrain.

My head is magnificently empty,
   my heart dangerously full;
my days are like tiny waves
   seen from a small bridge.

Perhaps my look is too tender
   for air that is barely warm.
I am already sick of summer –
   though hardly recovered from winter.

13 March 1915

13

Let me repeat, at the end of our love
   on the very eve of parting,
how much I loved those powerful
   hands of yours,

those eyes which do – or don't –
   look someone over, and
nevertheless demand a report
   on my most casual glance.

Three times is your passion cursed!
  God sees all of you
and insists on repentance
  for every casual sigh.

Now let me say again, wearily
  – don't be too eager to hear this –
your soul now stands
  in the way of my own.

And something else, since
  it is almost evening –
that mouth of yours was young
  when we first kissed,

your gaze was bold and light then
  your being – five years old...
How fortunate are those
  who have not crossed your path.

                                        28 April 1915

14

Some names are like sultry flowers
  and glances like dancing flames.
There are dark and sinuous mouths
  whose corners are deep and moist.

There are women with hair like helmets
  whose fans smell faintly of ruin.
They are thirty. Why would you need
  the soul of a Spartan child?

                            Annunciation Day 1915

15

I want to look in the mirror, where
  sleep is wrapped in mist.
I wonder where you are going
  and where you will find solace.

I see the mast of a ship
  with you on the deck,
or standing in the smoke of a train
  in the sad fields of evening.

There is dew on the night grass
  and above that – ravens.
I send you my blessings now
  to every corner of those fields

3 May 1915

16

At first, you loved beauty
  above everything, curls
with a delicate touch of henna,
  the melancholy sound of the *zurna*,

notes struck by a stallion's
  hooves against flint
or semi-precious stones
  with patterned facets.

In the next love, your second:
  an arch of fine eyebrows
and a silky carpet from
  rose-coloured Bokhara,

Every finger was ringed then,
    There was a birthmark on her cheek,
tanned flesh through Victorian
    lace – and London at midnight!

Your third love was sweet
    in some different way…
– But what trace remains in your heart
    of me, my faithless one?

                                        14 July 1915

                    ★

The clock – what time is it?
    The hour has sounded.
I can barely make out
    the hollows of huge eyes,
the flowing satin of your dress.
    I can barely see you.

Next door the lights are out.
    Someone is making love.
I am frightened by the
    shape of your face.
It is half dark in the room;
    Night is as lonely as if

a piece of ice pierced by moonlight
    marks the window.
– Did you surrender?
    I did not fight.
The voice froze as if from
    A hundred miles away or the moon itself

Moonbeams stood between us
   transforming the world.
The metal of your dark
   furiously red hair
glowed unbearably.
   History itself is forgotten,

in the flint of the moon, the looking glass
   splinters: there are distant hooves,
and the squeak of a carriage. The street light
   has gone out. Time no longer moves.
Soon the cock will crow. And two
   young women will part.

1 November 1914

Your narrow, foreign shape

Your narrow, foreign shape
  is bent above written pages,
with a Turkish shawl, dropped
  over you like a cloak.

You make a single line, which
  is broken and black at once.
And you are cold – in erotic
  gaiety – or unhappiness.

All your life is a fever to be
  perfected, yet this young
demon, who on earth is she
  with her cloudy, dark face?

Everyone else is worldly,
  while you remain playful,
with harmless lines of poetry –
  trifles – aimed at the heart.

In a sleepy, morning hour –
  at five a.m. – I discover
I've fallen in love with you,
  Anna Akhmatova

1915

I know the truth

I know the truth – give up all other truths!
No need for people anywhere on earth to struggle.
Look – it is evening, look, it is nearly night:
what do you speak of, poets, lovers, generals?

The wind is level now, the earth is wet with dew,
the storm of stars in the sky will turn to quiet.
And soon all of us will sleep under the earth, we
who never let each other sleep above it.

1915

What is this gypsy passion for separation

What is this gypsy passion for separation, this
   readiness to rush off – when we've just met?
My head rests in my hands as I
   realise, looking into the night

that no one turning over our letters has
   yet understood how completely and
how deeply faithless we are, which is
   to say: how true we are to ourselves.

1915

We shall not escape Hell

We shall not escape Hell, my passionate
sisters, we shall drink black resins –
we who sang our praises to the Lord
with every one of our sinews, even the finest,

we did not lean over cradles or
spinning wheels at night, and now we are
carried off by an unsteady boat
under the skirts of a sleeveless cloak,

we dressed every morning in
fine Chinese silk, and we would
sing our paradisal songs at
the fire of the robbers' camp,

slovenly needlewomen (all
our sewing came apart), dancers,
players upon pipes: we have been
the queens of the whole world!

first scarcely covered by rags,
then with constellations in our hair, in
gaol and at feasts we have
bartered away heaven,

in starry nights, in the apple
orchards of Paradise.
– Gentle girls, my beloved sisters,
we shall certainly find ourselves in Hell!

1915

Some ancestor of mine

Some ancestor of mine was a violinist
    and a thief into the bargain.
Does this explain my vagrant disposition
    and hair that smells of the wind?

Dark, curly-haired, hooknosed, he is
    the one who steals apricots
from the cart, using my hand. Yes,
    he is responsible for my fate.

Admiring the ploughman at his labour,
    he used to twirl a dog rose
in his lips. He was always unreliable
    as a friend, but a tender lover.

Fond of his pipe, the moon, beads, and all
    the young women in the neighbourhood…
I think he may have also been a coward,
    my yellow-eyed ancestor.

His soul was sold for a farthing,
    so he did not walk at midnight
in the cemetery. He may have worn
    a knife tucked in his boot.

Perhaps he pounced round corners
    like a sinuous cat.
I wonder suddenly: did
    he even play the violin?

I know nothing mattered to him
    any more than last year's snow.
That's what he was like, my ancestor.
    And that's the kind of poet I am.

1915

I'm glad your sickness

I'm glad your sickness is not caused by me.
Mine is not caused by you. I'm glad to know
the heavy earth will never flow away
from us, beneath our feet, and so
we can relax together, and not watch
our words. When our sleeves touch
we shall not drown in waves of rising blush.

I'm glad to see you calmly now embrace
another girl in front of me, without
any wish to cause me pain, as you
don't burn if I kiss someone else.
I know you never use my tender name,
my tender spirit, day or night. And
no one in the silence of a church
will sing their Hallelujahs over us.

Thank you for loving me like this,
for you feel love, although you do not know it.
Thank you for the nights I've spent in quiet.
Thank you for the walks under the moon
you've spared me and those sunset meetings unshared.
Thank you. The sun will never bless our heads.
Take my sad thanks for this: you do not cause
my sickness. And I don't cause yours.

1915

We are keeping an eye on the girls

We are keeping an eye on the girls, so that the *kvass*
doesn't go sour in the jug, or the pancakes cold,
counting over the rings, and pouring *anis*
into the long bottles with their narrow throats,

straightening tow thread for the peasant woman:
filling the house with the fresh smoke of
incense   and we are sailing over Cathedral Square
arm in arm with our godfather, silks thundering.

The wet nurse has a screeching cockerel
in her apron – her clothes are like the night.
She announces in an ancient whisper that
a dead young man   lies in the chapel.

And an incense cloud wraps the corners
under its own saddened chasuble.
The apple trees are white, like angels – and
the pigeons on them – grey – like incense itself.

And the pilgrim women sipping *kvass* from the ladle
on the edge of the couch, is telling
to the very end a tale about Razin
and his most beautiful Persian girl.

1916

No one has taken anything away

No one has taken anything away –
  there is even a sweetness for me in being apart.
I kiss you now across the many
  hundreds of miles that separate us.

I know: our gifts are unequal, which is
  why my voice is – quiet, for the first time.
What can my untutored verse
  matter to you, a young Derzhavin?

For your terrible flight I give you blessing.
  Fly, then, young eagle! You
have stared into the sun without blinking.
  Can my young gaze be too heavy for you?

No one has ever stared more
  tenderly or more fixedly after you…
I kiss you – across hundreds of
  separating years.

1916

You throw back your head

You throw back your head, because
you are proud. And a braggart.
This February has
brought me a gay companion!

Clattering with gold pieces, and
slowly puffing out smoke, we
walk like solemn foreigners
throughout my native city.

And whose attentive hands have
touched your eyelashes, beautiful boy, and
when or how many times your
lips have been kissed

I do not ask. That dream my thirsty
spirit has conquered. Now
I can honour in you the
divine boy, ten years old!

Let us wait by the river that
rinses the coloured beads of street-lights:
I shall take you as far as the square
that has witnessed adolescent Tsars.

Whistle out your boyish
pain, your heart squeezed in your hand.
My indifferent and crazy creature –
now set free – goodbye!

1916

Where does this tenderness come from?

Where does this tenderness come from?
These are not the – first curls I
have stroked slowly – and lips I
have known are – darker than yours

as stars rise often and go out again
(where does this tenderness come from?)
so many eyes have risen and died out
    in front of these eyes of mine,

and yet no such song have
I heard in the darkness of night before,
(where does this tenderness come from?):
    here, on the ribs of the singer.

Where does this tenderness come from?
And what shall I do with it, young
sly singer, just passing by?
Your lashes are – longer than anyone's.

1916

Bent with worry

Bent with worry, God
   paused, to smile.
And look, there were many
holy angels with bodies of

the radiance he had
   given them,
some with enormous wings and
others without any,

which is why I weep
   so much
because even more than God
himself I love his fair angels.

1916

Today or tomorrow the snow will melt

Today or tomorrow the snow will melt.
You lie alone beneath an enormous fur.
Shall I pity you? Your lips
have gone dry for ever.

Your drinking is difficult, your step heavy.
Every passer-by hurries away from you.
Was it with fingers like yours that Rogozhin
clutched the kitchen knife?

And the eyes, the eyes in your face!
Two circles of charcoal, year-old circles!
Surely when you were still young your girl
lured you into a joyless house.

Far away – in the night – over asphalt – a cane.
Doors – swing open into – night – under beating wind.
Come in! Appear! Undesired guest! Into
my chamber which is – most bright!

1916

VERSES ABOUT MOSCOW

1

There are clouds – about us
and domes – about us:
over the whole of Moscow
so many hands are needed!
I lift you up like a
sapling, my best burden: for
to me you are   weightless.

In this city of wonder
this peaceful city
I shall be joyful, even
when I am dead. You
shall reign, or grieve
or perhaps receive my crown:
for you are my first born!

When you fast – in Lent
do not blacken your brows
and honour the churches – these
forty times forty – go
about on foot – stride youthfully
over the whole seven of
these untrammelled hills.

Your turn will come.
You will give Moscow
with tender bitterness
to your daughter also.

As for me – unbroken sleep
and the sound of bells
in the surly dawn of
the Vagankovo cemetery.

Strange and beautiful brother – take this
city no hands built – out of my hands!

Church by church – all the forty times forty, and
the small pigeons also that rise over them.

Take the Spassky gate, with its flowers, where
the orthodox remove their caps, and

the chapel of stars, that refuge from evil,
where the floor is – polished by kisses.

Take from me the incomparable circle
of five cathedrals, ancient, holy friend!

I shall lead you as a guest from another
country to the Chapel of the Inadvertent Joy

where pure gold domes will begin to shine
for you, and sleepless bells will start thundering.

There the Mother of God will drop her
cloak upon you from the crimson clouds

and you will rise up filled with wonderful powers.
Then, you will not repent that you have loved me!

5

Over the city that great Peter rejected
rolls out the thunder of the bells.

A thundering surf has overturned upon
this woman you have now rejected.

I offer homage to Peter and you also,
yet above you both the bells remain

and while they thunder from that blueness, the
primacy of Moscow cannot be questioned

for all the forty times forty churches
laugh above the arrogance of Tsars.

7

There are seven hills – like seven bells
seven bells, seven bell-towers. Every
one of the forty times forty churches, and the
seven hills of bells have been numbered.

On a day of bells I was born, it was
the golden day of John the Divine.
The house was gingerbread surrounded by
wattle-fence, and small churches with gold heads.

And I loved it, I loved the first ringing,
the nuns flowing towards Mass, and
the wailing in the stone, the heat of sleeping –
the sense of a soothsayer in the neighbouring house.

Come with me, people of Moscow, all of you,
imbecile, thieving, flagellant mob!
And priest: stop my mouth up firmly
with Moscow – which is a land of bells!

8

Moscow, what a vast
hostelry is your house!
Everyone in Russia is — homeless,
we shall all make our way towards you.

With shameful brands on our backs and
knives — stuck in the tops of our boots,
for you call us in to you
however far away we are,

because for the brand of the criminal
and for every known sickness
we have our healer here,
the Child Panteleimon.

Behind a small door where
people pour in their crowds
lies the Iversky heart —
red-gold and radiant

and a Hallelujah floods
over the burnished fields.
Moscow soil, I bend to
kiss your breast.

1916

from *INSOMNIA*

2

As I love to
    kiss hands, and
to name everything, I
    love to open
doors!
        Wide – into the night!

Pressing my head
    as I listen to some
heavy step grow softer
    or the wind shaking
the sleepy and sleepless
        woods.

Ah, night
    small rivers of water rise
and bend towards – sleep.
    (I am nearly sleeping.)
Somewhere in the night a
    human being is drowning.

3

In my enormous city it is – night,
as from my sleeping house I go – out,
and people think perhaps I'm a daughter or wife
but in my mind is one thought only: night.

The July wind now sweeps a way for – me.
From somewhere, some window, music though – faint.
The wind can blow until the dawn – today,
in through the fine walls of the breast rib-cage.

Black poplars, windows, filled with – light.
Music from high buildings, in my hand a flower.
Look at my steps – following – nobody.
Look at my shadow, nothing's here of me.

The lights – are like threads of golden beads
in my mouth is the taste of the night – leaf.
Liberate me from the bonds of – day,
my friends, understand: I'm nothing but your dream.

5

Now as a guest from heaven, I
   visit your country:
I have seen the vigil of the forests
   and sleep in the fields.

Somewhere in the night horseshoes
   have torn up the grass, and
there are cows breathing heavily in
   a sleepy cowshed.

Now let me tell you sadly and
   with tenderness of the
goose-watchman awake, and
   the sleeping geese,

of hands immersed in dog's wool,
   grey hair – a grey dog –
and how towards six
   the dawn is beginning.

6

Tonight – I am alone in the night,
  a homeless and sleepless nun!
Tonight I hold all the keys to this
  the only capital city

and lack of sleep guides me on my path.
  You are so lovely, my dusky Kremlin!
Tonight I put my lips to the breast
  of the whole round and warring earth.

Now I feel hair – like fur – standing on end:
  the stifling wind blows straight into my soul.
Tonight I feel compassion for everyone,
  those who are pitied, along with those who are kissed.

7

In the pine-tree, tenderly tenderly,
  finely finely: something hissed.
It is a child with black
  eyes that I see in my sleep.

From the fair pine-trees hot
  resin drips, and in this
splendid night there are
  saw-teeth going over my heart.

8

Black as – the centre of an eye, the centre, a blackness
that sucks at light. I love your vigilance

Night, first mother of songs, give me the voice to sing of you
in those fingers lies the bridle of the four winds.

Crying out, offering words of homage to you, I am
only a shell where the ocean is still sounding.

But I have looked too long into human eyes.
Reduce me now to ashes – Night, like a black sun.

9

Who sleeps at night? No one is sleeping.
    In the cradle a child is screaming.
An old man sits over his death, and anyone
    young enough talks to his love, breathes
into her lips, looks into her eyes.

Once asleep – who knows if we'll wake again?
We have time, we have time, we have time to sleep!

From house to house the sharp-eyed
    watchman goes with his pink lantern
and over the pillow scatters the rattle
    of his loud clapper, rumbling.

Don't sleep! Be firm! Listen, the alternative
is – everlasting sleep. Your – everlasting house!

10

Here's another window
with more sleepless people!
Perhaps – drinking wine or
perhaps only sitting,
or maybe two lovers are
unable to part hands.
Every house has
a window like this.

A window at night: cries
of meeting or leaving.
Perhaps – there are many lights,
perhaps – only three candles.
But there is no peace in
my mind anywhere, for
in my house also, these
things are beginning:

Pray for the wakeful house,
friend, and the lit window.

1916

POEMS FOR AKHMATOVA

1

Muse of lament, you are the most beautiful of
   all muses, a crazy emanation of white night:
and you have sent a black snow storm over all Russia.
   We are pierced with the arrows of your cries

so that we shy like horses at the muffled
   many times uttered pledge – Ah! – Anna
Akhmatova – the name is a vast sigh
and it falls into depths without name

and we wear crowns only through stamping
   the same earth as you, with the same sky over us.
Whoever shares the pain of your deathly power will
   lie down immortal – upon his death bed.

In my melodious town the domes are burning
   and the blind wanderer praises our shining Lord.
I give you my town of many bells,
   Akhmatova, and with the gift: my heart.

2

I stand   head in my hands   thinking how
    unimportant are the traps we set for one another.
I hold my head in my hands   as I sing
    in this late hour, in the late dawn.

Ah how violent is this wave which has
    lifted me up on to its crest: I sing
of one   that is unique among us
    as the moon is   alone in the sky,

that has flown into my heart like a raven,
    has speared into the clouds
hook-nosed, with deathly anger: even
    your favour is   dangerous,

for you have spread out your night
    over the pure gold of my Kremlin itself
and have tightened my throat with the pleasure
    of singing   as if with a strap.

Yes, I am happy, the dawn never
    burnt with more purity, I am
happy to give everything to you
    and to go away   like a beggar,

for I was the first to give you –
    whose voice   deep darkness!   has
constricted the movement of my breathing –
    the name of the Tsarskoselsky Muse.

3

I am a convict. You won't fall behind.
You are my guard. Our fate is therefore one.
And in that emptiness that we both share
the same command to ride away is given.

And now my demeanour is calm.
And now   my eyes are without guile.
Won't you set me free, my guard, and
let me walk now, towards that pine-tree?

4

You block out everything, even the sun
    at its highest, hold all the stars in your hand!
If only through – some wide open door, I
    could blow like the wind to where you are,

and starting to stammer, suddenly blushing,
    could lower my eyes before you
and fall quiet, in tears, as
    a child sobs to receive forgiveness.

1916

POEMS FOR BLOK

1

Your name is a – bird in my hand
a piece of – ice on the tongue
one single movement of the lips.
Your name is: five signs,
a ball caught in flight, a
silver bell in the mouth

a stone, cast in a quiet pool
makes the splash of your name, and
the sound is in the clatter of
night hooves, loud as a thunderclap
or it speaks straight into my forehead,
shrill as the click of a cocked gun.

Your name – how impossible, it
is a kiss in the eyes on
motionless eyelashes, chill and sweet.
Your name is a kiss of snow
a gulp of icy spring water, blue
as a dove. About your name is: sleep.

1916

2

Tender – spectre
blameless as a knight, who
has called you into
my adolescent life?

In blue dark, grey
and priestly, you
stand here, dressed in snow.

And it's not the wind
that drives me through the town now.
No, this is the third
night I felt the old enemy.

With light blue eyes his
magic has bound
me, that snowy singer:

swan of snow, under
my feet he spreads his feathers.
Hovering feathers,
slowly they dip in the snow.

Thus upon feathers
I go, towards the door
behind which is: death.

He sings to me
behind the blue windows.
He sings to me
as jewelled bells.

Long is the shout from
his swan's beak as
he calls.

Dear spectre of
mist I know this is dreaming,
so one favour now, do
for me, amen: of dispersing.
Amen, amen.

1916

3

You are going – west of the sun now.
You will see there – evening light.
You are going – west of the sun and
snow will cover up your tracks.

Past my windows – passionless
you are going in quiet snow.
Saint of God, beautiful, you
are the quiet light of my soul

but I do not long for your spirit.
Your way is indestructible.
And your hand is pale from holy
kisses, no nail of mine.

By your name I shall not call you.
My hands shall not stretch after you
to your holy waxen face I shall
only bow – from afar

standing under the slow falling snow, I shall
fall to my knees – in the snow.
In your holy name I shall only
kiss that evening snow

where, with majestic pace you
go by in tomb-like quiet,
the light of quiet – holy glory
of it: keeper of my soul.

1916

5

At home in Moscow – where the domes are burning,
at home in Moscow – in the sound of bells,
where I live the tombs – in their rows are standing
and in them Tsaritsas – are asleep and Tsars.

And you don't know how – at dawn the Kremlin is
the easiest place to – breathe in the whole wide earth
and you don't know when – dawn reaches the Kremlin
I pray to you until – the next day comes

and I go with you – by your river Neva
even while beside – the Moscow river
I am standing here – with my head lowered
and the line of street lights – sticks fast together.

With my insomnia – I love you wholly.
With my insomnia – I listen for you,
just at the hour throughout – the Kremlin, men
who ring the bells – begin to waken.

Still my river – and your river
still my hand – and your hand
will never join, or not until
one dawn catches up another dawning.

1916

8

And the gadflies gather about indifferent cart-horses,
the red calico of Kaluga puffs out in the wind,
it is a time of whistling quails and huge skies,
bells waving over waves of corn, and more
talk about Germans than anyone can bear.
Now yellow, yellow, beyond the blue trees is a
cross, and a sweet fever, a radiance over
everything: *your name*   sounding like *angel.*

1916

9

A weak shaft of light through the blackness of hell is
your voice under the rumble of exploding shells

in that thunder like a seraph he is announcing
in a toneless voice, from somewhere else, some

ancient misty morning he inhabits, how he
loved us, who are blind and nameless   who

share the blue cloak of sinful treachery
and more tenderly than anyone loved the woman who

sank more daringly than any into the night   of evil,
and of his love for you, Russia, which he cannot end.

And he draws an absent-minded finger along
his temple   all the time he tells us of

the days that wait for us, how God will deceive us.
We shall call for the sun and it will not rise.

He spoke like a solitary prisoner
(or perhaps a child speaking to himself)

so that over the whole square the sacred
heart of Alexander Blok appeared to us.

1920

6

Thinking him   human   they
decided to kill him, and
now he's dead. For ever.
– Weep. For the dead angel.

At the day's setting, he
sang the evening beauty.
Three waxen lights now
shudder superstitiously

and lines of light, hot
strings across the snow come from him.
Three waxen candles.
To the sun. The light-bearer.

O now look how
dark his eyelids are fallen,
O now look how
his wings are broken.

The black reciter reads.
The people idly stamp.
Dead lies the singer, and
celebrates resurrection.

1916

Look there he is, weary from foreign parts,
a leader without body-guard

there – he is drinking a mountain stream from his hands
a prince without native land.

He has everything in his holy princedom there
Army, bread and mother.

Lovely is your inheritance.
Govern, friend without friends.

1921

A kiss on the head

A kiss on the head – wipes away misery.
I kiss your head.

A kiss on the eyes – takes away sleeplessness.
I kiss your eyes.

A kiss on the lips – quenches the deepest thirst.
I kiss your lips.

A kiss on the head – wipes away memory.
I kiss your head.

1917

from *SWANS' ENCAMPMENT*

Little mushroom, white Bolitus,
                    my own favourite
The field sways, a chant of 'Rus'
                    rises over it.
Help me, I'm unsteady on my feet.
This blood-red is making my eyes foggy.

On either side, mouths lie
open and bleeding, and from
each wound rises a cry:
— Mother!

One word is all I hear, as
I stand dazed. From someone
else's womb   into my own:
— Mother!

They all lie in a row,
no line between them,
I recognise that each one was a soldier.
But which is mine? Which one is another's?

This man was White   now he's become Red.
Blood has reddened him.
This one was Red   now he's become White.
Death has whitened him.

— What are you? White? — Can't understand!
                    — Lean on your arm!
Have you been with the Reds?
                    — Ry   -azan.

And so from right and left
Behind   ahead
together, White and Red, one cry of
– Mother!

Without choice. Without anger.
One long moan. Stubbornly.
A cry that reaches up to heaven,
– Mother!

1917–21

Yesterday he still looked in my eyes

Yesterday he still looked in my eyes, yet
    today   his looks are bent aside.   Yesterday
he sat here until the birds began, but
    today   all those larks are   ravens.

Stupid creature! And you are wise, you
    live while I am stunned.
Now for the lament of women in all times:
– My love, what was it I did to you?

And tears are   water, blood is   water,
    a woman always washes in blood and tears.
Love is a step-mother, and no mother:
    then expect no justice or mercy from her.

Ships carry away the ones we love.
    Along the white road they are taken away.
And one cry stretches across the earth:
    – My love, what was it I did to you?

Yesterday he lay at my feet. He even
    compared me to the Chinese empire! Then
suddenly he let his hands fall open, and
    my life fell out like   a rusty kopeck.

A child-murderer, before some court
    I stand   loathsome and timid I am.
And yet even in Hell I shall demand:
    – My love, what was it I did to you?

I ask this chair, I ask the bed: Why?
    Why do I suffer and live in penury?
His kisses stopped. He wanted to break you.
    To kiss another girl is their reply.

He taught me to live in fire, he threw me there,
　　and then abandoned me on steppes of ice.
My love, I know what you have done to me.
　　　– My love, what was it I did to you?

I know everything, don't argue with me!
　　I can see now, I'm a lover no longer.
And now I know wherever love holds power
　　Death approaches soon　　like a gardener.

It is almost like shaking a tree, in time
　　some ripe apple comes falling down. So
for everything, for everything　　forgive me,
　　　– my love　　whatever it was I did to you.

1920

To Mayakovsky

High above cross and trumpet
baptised in smoke and fire
my clumsy-footed angel –
Hello there, Vladimir!

Carter and horse at once
justice and whim together.
He used to spit on his palms –
Hold on, carthorse of glory!

Singer of gutter miracles,
grubby, arrogant friend –
Hullo there, you who prefer
topaz to diamond!

Now yawn, play your trump card
my thunderbolt of cobbles,
and rake this horse's shaft
once more with your angel wing.

1921

ON A RED HORSE

No Muse – I had no Muse
to sing by my shabby cradle,
no Muse to warm my hands
or cool my feverish eyelids.
No Muse – combed the hair from my face,
No Muse – led me into the fields.

There was no Muse. No braids,
no beads, no fables – only
tufts of brown hair cut
short over male eyebrows:
a figure in full armour.
A sultan.

He did not lean over my lips.
He did not bless me at bedtime,
still less, grieve with me over
a broken doll. Instead,
he set all my birds free.
On a red horse, he rode off
with pitiless spurs over
navy blue mountains
into a thundering blizzard.

★

Firemen! – A scream
wide as the blaze – *Firemen!*
Is that our house burning? –
No, a soul is on fire!

Loudly, the tongue of alarm bells
swings backward and forward –
a soul makes a huge fire –
Firemen! My soul is burning

in a dance of fierce beauty,
red torches woven together.
Applause – screams – whistles.
A roar as sparks scatter.

I am lost in a dream
and can't wake up. I'm only
wearing a nightdress –
ankle length – and a necklace.

Listen to the flames howl,
and the sound of glass shattering.
Our eyes are glowing orbs.
We are burning   burning   burning.

Firemen! Who cries arson?
Who wants the fire to go out?
I long for these supporting
girders to collapse.

But what is being destroyed here?
Not columns, but desperate hands,
small hands held up to the sky –
I recognise my doll.

Who races in at a gallop?
Who jumps off a red horse?
With a haughty glance at me,
he enters the red house.

Another cry. Louder still.
A cry, and a thunderous blow
He holds up the doll like a shell
And rises like fire itself.

Like the Tsar, among surging flames
he declares with a frown: *I saved her*
for you.   *Now smash her...*
Let your love go.

And has the world collapsed?
What approaches through the blizzard?
Two arms – stretched after the horse –
The girl – without – her doll.

★

An evil moon through the window:
I am dreaming again.

My lover and I stand close
in a deep embrace. Below us,
the noisy flow of a river.
The foam reaches up to our feet.

Speechless in our embrace
we observe the splashing foam.
I – am all his harems.
He – all my knightly heroes.

We stand, closely holding each other.
Side by side, hand in hand,
The foam reaches our feet.
Then I suddenly ask him to swear

that if I should drop a flower
or a scarf, from the bridge,
he would dive into the river…
To my horror, he does so at once.

I am left on the bridge, shaking,
My blood moans as I see
in terror – dumbly – watching:
my whole life drowning with him.

Now who with the sweep of a cloak
has thrown me up in the air?
Who is it – splashed with red –
throws me into a fire?

With a splash, and triumphant cry
in a smooth jump out of the water
he rises like the river itself
with a body in his arms

like a Tsar in the midst of the surges
he rises to say with a frown
I saved him for you. Now kill him!
Let your love go!

And now what moves in the blizzard?
Two arms – stretching – after
the man on a red horse.
The girl – without – her lover.

★

Now through the window crack
I dream another dream.

Darkness over a track,
and I am with my son.
The blood congeals in my veins.
Let some guide lead us on!

Be brave, my child, the spirit
of the mountain is single.
Only eagles, and Dawn here
– while there are two of us.

A whirlwind! Gods would turn back.
Eagles would be afraid. But
my firstborn inches higher.
We shall reach the heights together.

That's why I had a son, in pain,
in the dust of the earth, so that
from under an eagle's wing
this should be mine – God's thunder.

Black height.   Barren slope.
Handholds for small hands.
Is that Zeus above us in his cot
holding an eagle?

Laughter – a violent splash.
Some creature with wings and claws.
Who is pursuing me – with lightning
and eagle thunder?

A hoarse roar splits wide open
The stony breast of the mountain.
Lifting my child like his own,
look, the Rider is rising

like the Tsar among surging clouds
he stands, with a frown on his face.
I saved him for you – now kill him!
Let your love go!

What suddenly cracked? Was it
a dry tree?   No.   Two arms
stretch toward the horse.
A girl – has lost – motherhood.

★

An evil dawn through the window crack
I dream my third dream.

February.   Crooked roads.
The snowstorm in the fields
sweeps across wide tracks –
a whole tribe of winds.

I'm hopping over a slope
and then – up a steep mountain.
I'm following *red*, a red horse.
We are taking the same track.

For a moment – he's there,
within hand's reach and taunting:
Touch me. My hands find
nothing… Ahead, only horse and snow.

Winds, pile drifts on doorways!
cover the steep cliffs over
so that at last the red horse
has to stop dead in his tracks.

★

And now it's not the blizzard
but a broom sweeps me away,
not the stroke of a sultan
but an old hag with grey

dishevelled hair and her nose
deep in the steam of a cauldron.
She has a rag in her hand,
and a covered decanter

with a glass, which at first
she sets aside – then sips
– What does it mean, my dream?
– *Your Angel doesn't love you!*

A crack of thunder, that –
A crowbar on the skull.
My heads sinks into the pillow
I repeat *He doesn't love me.*

Doesn't love me? No need for braids, then.
Doesn't love me? Or a necklace.
Doesn't love me? I'll mount a horse,
and ride off into battle.

★

Soldiers, who are we fighting?
A cold flame enters my chest
like a steel lance, a light beam
pierces under my breast.

And he whispers *I wanted this.*
It is for this I chose you,
you are my passion, my sister,
mine till the end of time

my bride of ice – in armour –
Mine. Will you stay with me
and belong to no one else?
With a hand on my wound, I agree.

So – not the Muse, not the Muse.
Not the ties of kinship which perish
not the fetters men call friendship
and not by a woman's hand.

What tightens on me is a fierce
knot. This union frightens.
I am in a ditch, in darkness
even as dawn lightens.

Who attached these heavy wings
on my shoulders? I am
a witness of living storm –
someone who sees shadows,

until I am carried high
into the blue above us
at last – on a red horse –
by my own Genius!

13–17 January 1921

Praise to the Rich

And so, making clear in advance
I know there are miles   between us;
and I reckon myself with the tramps, which
is a place of honour in this world:

under the wheels of luxury, at
table with cripples and hunchbacks...
From the top of the bell-tower roof,
I proclaim it: I *love* the rich.

For their rotten, unsteady root
for the damage done in their cradle
for the absent-minded way their hands
go in and out of their pockets;

for the way their softest word is
obeyed like a shouted order; because
they will not be let into heaven; and
because they don't look in your eyes;

and because they send secrets   by courier!
and their passions   by errand boy.
In the nights that are thrust upon them they
kiss and drink under compulsion,

and because in all their accountings
in boredom, in gilding, in wadding,
they can't buy me   I'm too brazen:
I confirm it, I *love* the rich!

and in spite of their shaven fatness,
their fine drink   (wink, and spend):
some sudden   defeatedness
and a look that is like a dog's

doubting…
            the core of their balance
nought, but are the weights true?
I say that among all outcasts
there are no such orphans on earth.

There is also a nasty fable
about camels getting through needles
   for that look, surprised to death
apologizing for sickness, as

if they were suddenly bankrupt: 'I would have been
glad to lend, but'   and their silence.
I counted in carats once and then I was one of them.
For all these things, I swear it: I *love* the rich.

                               1922

God help us   Smoke!

God help us   Smoke!
– Forget that. Look at the damp.
These are the ordinary fears
    of anyone moving house

approaching a poor lamp
    for students in miserable outskirts.
– Isn't there even a tree
    for the children? What sort of landlord

will we have? Too strict?
    in a necklace of coins, a porter
impervious as fate
    to the shudder in our pockets.

What kind of neighbour?
    Unmarried? Perhaps not noisy?
The old place was no pleasure
    but still the air there breathed

our atmosphere, was soaked
    in our own odours. Easy,
to put up with fetid air
    if it isn't soiled by outsiders!

It was old, of course, and
    rotting, but still... Not a hostel room!
I don't know about being born
    but this is for dying in!

1922

Ophelia: In Defence of the Queen

Prince, let's have no more disturbing
    these wormy flower-beds. Look at
the living rose, and think of a woman
    snatching a single day – from the few left to her.

Prince Hamlet, you defile the Queen's
    womb. Enough. A virgin cannot
judge passion. Don't you know Phaedra
    was more guilty, yet men still sing of her,

and will go on singing. You, with your blend
    of chalk and rot, you bony
scandalmonger, how can you ever
    understand a fever in the blood?

Beware, if you continue… I can
    rise up through flagstones into the grand bed-chamber
of so much sweetness, I myself, to defend her.
    I myself – your own undying passion!

1923

from *WIRES*

Along these singing lines that run
from pole to pole, supporting heaven
I send along to you my portion
of earthly dust.
           From wires
to poles. This alley sighs
the telegraphic words: I lo-o-ve

I beg. (No printed form would
hold that word! But wires are simpler.)
Atlas himself upon these poles
lowered the racetrack
of the Gods.
           Along these files
The telegraphic word: g-oo-dbye...

Do you hear it? This last word
torn from my throat: *Forg-i-ve*...
Over these calm Atlantic fields
the rigging holds. And higher, higher.
All the messages fuse together
in Ariadne's web: *Ret-u-rn*...
and plaintive cries of: *I won't leave*...

These wires are steely guards upon
voices from Hell,

receding... far into that distance
still implored for some compassion.
Compassion? (But in such a chorus
can you distinguish such a noise?)
That cry, arising as death comes –
through mounds – and ditches – that last

65

waft of her — passion that persists —
Euridice's: *A-a-alas*

and not — a —

17 March 1923

2

If I spoke to you directly — not like this,
crushed into lines and rhymes —
but from my whole heart, even Racine
or Shakespeare could not cope with it!

Everyone wept, with poison in their blood.
They wept to see a snake among the roses.
But Phaedra had only one Hyppolitus,
and Ariadne only wept for Theseus —

while in losing you, I have lost
everything I love, I am adrift,
there is no shore, no boundary to pain —
everyone who ever lived is forfeit.

What can I hope for now? The very air
I breathe is so accustomed to you.
My own bones have grown into a prison,
lonely as Naxos — my blood is the Styx.

Vanity! In me — and everywhere!
To close my eyes against it has no meaning
— since there is no daylight — and besides
the date on the calendar is lying…

and when you — break off like this —
I am no Ariadne, no Phaedra.
Only *loss!*

Over which seas, in what cities
shall I look for you? (A blind
search for the invisible.) I must
rely on wires, and weep at every pole.

18 March 1923

3

Sorting through everything, throwing out
whatever I can, I reject first of all
the semaphore, that wildest discord
– though a whole chorus rushes to the rescue,

with sleeves like banners, still
I throw them all out – shamelessly.
A lyric drone of wires hums
above as if I were in traction.

The telegraph! Could we not communicate
more quickly? The sky is still above us,
a constant dispenser of emotion,
as tangible as lips…

The heavens arch above me
with dawn on the horizon,
even at this distance I can weave
a thread to reach you.

Across the harshest years of this epoch,
over disgusting piles of tackle and gear,
here fly my unpublished sighs
my raging passions – they are

simpler than a telegram (loyal, urgent
even hackneyed)   they will cross
the space between us   along
these wires   as gutters flood in spring.

19 March 1923

4

A camp of freedom!
Telegraph wires carry
this cry of passion from
my womb to the winds.

A magnetic spark from my heart
has torn these rhythms open:
'Metre and measure?' The fourth
dimension announces itself!

Hurry – over dead metres – and
over false witness – whistling!

Hush… when suddenly your head
begins to ache (there are wires
everywhere) you will recognise
all this obscure verbiage is only

the song of a strayed nightingale who sings
– *without the one you love the world is empty!* –
for the lyre in your hands, beloved,
and the Leila of your lips.

20 March 1923

5

Patiently, as tarmac under hammers,
patiently, as what is new matures,
patiently, as death must be awaited,
patiently, as vengeance may be nursed.

So I shall wait for you. (One look down to earth.
Cobblestones. Lips between. And numb.)
Patiently, as sloth can be prolonged,
patiently, as someone threading beads.

Toboggans squeak outside, the door answers
Now the wind's roar is inside the forest.
What has arrived is writing, whose corrections
are lofty as a change of reign, or a prince's entrance.

And let's go home!
This is inhuman —
yet it's mine.

25 March 1923

6

At the very hour my dearest brother
    passed beyond the last elm
(with a formal wave of the hand)
    my tears were larger than my eyes.

In the hour when my dearest friend
    sailed round the last Cape
(my whole being sighed: *Come back!*)
    and the wave of my hand stretched

after him — from my shoulders —
    my lips — followed — entreating
but my speech lost all sound,
    my hands lost their fingers.

This is the hour when we approach
    with gifts — nobler than the Tsars.
The hour when I come down the mountain.
    And the mountain understands.

Wishes have gathered in a circle.
    Destinies have shifted. Don't complain!
In this hour, hands are invisible.
    And souls begin to see.

In the hour when my dear guest
   left me – Look, look at us!
Our tears were larger than human
   eyes – and wider than the Atlantic

... – Stars!

26 March 1923

8

Wherever you are, I can reach you
to summon up – or send you back again!
Yet I'm no sorceress. My eyes grew sharp in
The white book of the distant River Don.

From the height of my cedar I see a world
where court decisions float, and all lights wander
yet from here I can turn the whole sea upside down
to bring you from its depths – or send you under!

You can't resist me. Since I'm everywhere
as daylight, underground, in breath and bread
I'm always present. That is how I shall procure
your lips – as God will surely claim your soul –

In your last breath, even in that choking hour
I'll be there at the great Archangel's fence
To put these bloodied lips up against the thorns
of Judgement – and to snatch you from your bier!

Surrender! This is no fairy tale
Surrender! Any arrow will fall back on you.
Surrender! Don't you know no one escapes
the power of creatures reaching out with

breath alone? (That's how I soar up
with my eyes shut and mica round my mouth.)
Be careful, the prophetess tricked Samuel.
Perhaps I'll hoodwink you. Return alone,

because another girl is with you. Now on Judgement Day
there'll be no litigation. So till then
I'll wander. And yet I'll have your soul
As an alchemist knows how to win your

lips...

27 March 1923

9

Spring makes us sleepy. So let's sleep.
    We are apart, but separation
can be healed by sleeping. Perhaps
    we may meet each other in a dream.

An all-seeing eye knows into whose
    hand I will next place my palm;
to whom I will reveal this sorrow
    and share my unhappiness

which is eternal (no child,
    no father expects it to end).
It is the misery of those who cry,
    without a shoulder to lean on,

about memory slipping through
    fingers, like a stone from a bridge...
about the way all places are taken,
    all hearts already rented.

It concerns serving – endlessly – having
    to live – without happiness –
written off – before recognition – in archives
    – that Paradise of the crippled –

it is about you and I, like quiet streams
    running deeper than precious metal –
about everything stitched by a seamstress:
    drudgery – drudgery – drudgery.

5 April 1923

10

With other people – in heaps
of roses – in bits of weeks
only guessed at…
                    I remain
yours, like a chosen bundle,

even as the wind picks me up
like sand or gravel, and the rails
– overhearing me – send my dust
out to breadless provinces.

Do you recognise this shawl? Hotter
than Hell gates when pulled across
a freezing body –
                    look, I fling it open.
Below the hem: the miracle of a child.

It is *Song* itself! And with this first-born,
greater than any Rachel, with –
my own imagination I dislodge
this stubborn sediment.

11 April 1923

Sahara

Young men, don't ride away! Sand
    stifled the soul of the
last one to disappear and now
    he's altogether dumb.

To look for him is useless.
    (Young men, I never lie.)
That lost one now reposes
    in a reliable grave.

He once rode into me as if
    through lands of
miracles and fire, with all
    the power of poetry, and

I was: dry, sandy, without day.
    He used poetry
to invade my depths, like those of
    any other country!

Listen to this story of two
    souls, without jealousy:
we entered one another's eyes
    as if they were oases –

I took him into me as if he were
    a god, in passion,
simply because of a charming tremor
    in his young throat.

Without a name he sank into me. But now
    he's gone. Don't search for him.
All deserts forget the thousands of
    those who sleep in them.

And afterwards the Sahara in one
  seething collapse will
cover you also with sand like sprinkled
  foam. And be your hill!

1923

The Poet

1

A poet's speech begins   a great way off.
A poet is   carried far away by speech

by way of planets, signs, and the   ruts
of roundabout parables, between *yes* and *no*,
in his hands even sweeping gestures from a bell-tower
become hook-like. For the way of comets

is the poet's way. And the blown–apart
links of causality   are his links. Look up
after him without hope. The eclipses of
poets are not foretold in the calendar.

He is the one that mixes up the cards
and confuses   arithmetic and weight,
demands answers from the school bench,
the one who altogether refutes Kant,

the one in the stone graves of the Bastille
who remains like a tree in its loveliness.
And yet the one whose   traces have always vanished,
the train everyone always arrives
too late to catch

                    for the path of comets
is the path of poets: they burn without warming,
pick without cultivating. They are: an explosion, a breaking in –
and the mane of their path makes the   curve of a
graph   cannot be foretold by the calendar.

2

There are superfluous people about in
this world, out of sight, who
aren't listed in any directory; and
home for them is   a rubbish heap.

They are hollow, jostled creatures:
who keep silent, dumb as dung, they are
nails   catching in your silken hem,
dirt   imagined under your wheels.

Here they are, ghostly and invisible, the
sign is on them, like the speck of the leper.
People like Job in this world who
might even have envied him. If.

We are poets, which has the sound of outcast.
Nevertheless, we step out from our shores.
We dare contend for godhead, with goddesses,
and for the Virgin   with the gods themselves.

Now what shall I do here, blind and fatherless?
Everyone else can see and has a father.
Passion in this world has to leap anathema
as it might be over the walls of a trench
and weeping   is called a cold in the head.

What shall I do, by nature and trade
a singing creature (like a wire – sunburn! Siberia!)
as I go over the bridge of my enchanted
visions, that cannot be weighed, in a
world that deals only in weights and measures?

What shall I do, singer and first-born, in a
world where the deepest black is grey,
and inspiration is kept in   a thermos?
with all this immensity
in a measured world?

1923

Appointment

I'll be late for the meeting
we arranged. When I arrive, my hair
will be grey. Yes, I suppose I grabbed
at spring. And you set your hopes much too high.

I shall walk with this bitterness for years
across mountains or town squares equally,
(Ophelia didn't flinch at rue!) I'll walk
on souls and on hands without shuddering.

Living on. As the earth continues.
With blood in every thicket, every creek.
Even though Ophelia's face is waiting
between the grasses bordering every stream.

She gulped at love, and filled her mouth
with silt. A shaft of light on metal!
I set my love upon you. Much too high.
In the sky   arrange my burial.

1923

Rails

The bed of a railway cutting
   has tidy sheets. The steel–blue
parallel tracks ruled out
   as neatly as staves of music.

And over them people are driven
   like possessed creatures from Pushkin
whose piteous song   has been silenced.
   Look, they're departing, deserting.

And yet lag behind and linger,
   the note of pain always rising
higher than love, as the poles freeze
   to the bank, like Lot's wife, forever.

Despair has appointed an hour for me
   (as someone arranges a marriage): then
Sappho with her voice gone
   I shall weep like a simple seamstress

with a cry of passive lament –
   a marsh heron! The moving train
will hoot its way over the sleepers
   and slice through them like scissors.

Colours blur in my eye,
   their glow a meaningless red.
All young women at times
   are tempted – by such a bed!

1923

You loved me

You loved me. And your lies had their own probity.
   There was a truth in every falsehood.
Your love went far beyond any possible
   boundary   as no one else's could.

Your love seemed to last even longer
   than time itself. Now you wave your hand –
and suddenly your   love for me is over!
   That is the truth in five words.

1923

It's not like waiting for post

It's not like waiting for post.
This is how you wait for
the one letter you need:
soft stuff bound with
tape and paste.
Inside a little word.
That's all. Happiness.

Waiting for happiness?
It's more like waiting for death.
The soldiers will salute
and three chunks of lead
will slam into your chest.
Your eyes will then flash red.

No question of joy.
Too old now, all bloom gone.
Waiting for what else now but
black muzzles in a square yard.

A square letter. I think
there may be spells in the ink.
No hope. And no one is
too old to face death

     or such a square envelope.

1923

My ear attends to you

My ear attends to you,
as a mother hears in her sleep.
To a feverish child, she whispers
as I bend over you.

At the skin, my blood calls out to
your heart, my whole sky craves
an island of tenderness.
My rivers tilt towards you.

And I am drawn downwards
as stairs slope into a garden,
or some willow's bough falls
straight down, away from the milestone.

Stars are pulled to the earth
and laurels on graves won
with suffering, attract banners.
An owl longs for a hollow.

And I lean down
towards you with muscle and wing,
as if to a grave stone,
(I put the years to sleep)

my lips seek yours... like spring.

1923

As people listen intently

As people listen intently
    (a river's mouth to its source)
that's how they smell a flower
to the depths, till they lose all sense.

That's how they feel their deepest
    craving in dark air,
as children lying in blue sheets
peer into memory.

And that's how a young boy feels
when his blood begins to change.
    When people fall in love with love
they fling themselves in the abyss.

1923

Strong doesn't mate with strong

Strong doesn't mate with strong.
It's not allowed in this world.
So Siegfried missed Brünnhilde,
in marriage fixed by a sword.

Like buffaloes, stone on stone,
in brotherly hatred joined,
he left their marriage bed, unknown,
she slept, unrecognised.

Apart, in the marriage bed.
Apart, in ambiguous language.
Apart, and clenched like a fist.
Too late.   And apart.   That's marriage.

More ancient evil yet:
Achilles, Thetis' son
crushing the Amazon
like a lion, missed Penthesilea.

Think of her glance, when felled
from her horse in the mud,
she looked up at him then
and not down from Olympus.

And afterwards, his passion was
to snatch his wife back from darkness?
But equal never mates with equal.

And so, we missed each other.

1924

In a world

In a world where most people
are hunched and sweaty
I know only one person
equal to me in strength.

In a world where there is
so much to want
I know only one person
equal to me in power.

In a world where mould
and ivy cover everything
I know only one person – you –
who equals me in spirit.

1924

POEM OF THE MOUNTAIN

Liebster, Dich wundert
die Rede? Alle Scheidenden
reden wie Trunkene und
nehmen sich festlich...

Hölderlin

A shudder: off my shoulders
   with this mountain! My soul rises.
Now let me sing of sorrow which
   is my own mountain

a blackness which I will
   never block out again:
Let me sing of sorrow
   from the top of the mountain!

1

A mountain, like the body of
a recruit mown down by shells,
wanting lips that were
unkissed, and a wedding ceremony

the mountain demanded those.
Instead, an ocean broke into its ears
with sudden shouts of hooray! Though
the mountain fought and struggled.

The mountain was like thunder!
A chest drummed on by Titans.
(Do you remember that last house
of the mountain – the end of the suburb?)

The mountain was many worlds!
And God took a high price for one.
Sorrow began with a mountain.
This mountain looked on the town.

2

Not Parnassus   not Sinai
simply a bare and military
hill. Form up! Fire!
Why is it then in my eyes
(since it was October and not May)
that mountain was Paradise?

3

On an open hand Paradise was offered,
(if it's too hot, don't even touch it!)
threw itself under our feet with all
its gullies and steep crags,

with paws of Titans, with all
its shrubbery and pines
the mountain seized the skirts of our
coats, and commanded: stop.

How far from schoolbook Paradise
it was: so *windy*, when
the mountain pulled us down on our
backs. To itself. Saying: lie here!

The violence of that pull bewildered us.
How? Even now I don't know.
Mountain. Pimp. For holiness.
It pointed, to say: here.

4

How to forget Persephone's pomegranate
seed in the coldness of winter?
I remember lips half-opening to
mine, like the valves of a shell-creature

lost because of that seed, Persephone!
Continuous as the redness of lips,
and your eyelashes   were like jagged points
upon the golden angles of a star.

Not that passion is   deceitful or imaginary!
It doesn't lie. Simply, it doesn't last!
If only we could come into this world as though
we were common people in love

be sensible, see things as they are: this
is just a hill, just a bump in the ground.
(And yet they say it is by the pull of
an abyss, that you measure height.)

In the heaps of gorse, coloured dim
among islands of tortured pines…
(In delirium above the level of
life)
        – Take me then. I'm yours.

Instead only the gentle mercies of
domesticity – chicks twittering –
because we came down into this world who
once lived at the height of heaven: in love.

The mountain was mourning (and mountains do mourn,
their clay is bitter, in the hours of parting).
The mountain mourned: for the tenderness
(like doves) of our undiscovered mornings.

The mountain mourned: for our friendliness, for
that unbreakable kinship of the lips.
The mountain declared that everyone will
receive in proportion to his tears.

The mountain grieved because   life is a gypsy-camp,
and we go marketing all our life from heart to heart.
And this was Hagar's grief. To be
sent far away. Even with her child.

Also the mountain said that all things were a trick
of some demon, no sense to the game.
The mountain sorrowed. And we were silent,
leaving the mountain to judge the case.

The mountain mourned for what is now blood
and heat will turn only to sadness.
The mountain mourned. It will not let us go.
It will not let you lie with someone else!

The mountain mourned, for what is now
world and Rome will turn   only to smoke.
The mountain mourned, because we shall be with
others. (And I do not envy them!)

The mountain mourned: for the terrible load
of promises, too late for us to renounce.
The mountain mourned the ancient nature of
the Gordian knot of law and passion.

The mountain mourned for our mourning also.
For tomorrow! Not yet! Above our foreheads
will break – death's sea of – memories!
For tomorrow, when we shall realise!

That sound   what?   as if someone were
crying just nearby? Can that be it?
The mountain is mourning. Because we must go down
separately, over such mud,

into life which we all know is nothing but
mob market barracks:
That sound said: all poems of
mountains   are written   *thus*

8

Hump of Atlas, groaning
    Titan, this town where we
live, day in, day out, will come
    to take a pride in the mountain

where we defeated life – at cards, and
    insisted with passion *not to*
exist. Like a bear-pit.
    And the twelve apostles.

Pay homage to my dark cave,
    (I was a cave that the waves entered).
The last hand of the card game was
    played, you remember, at the edge of the suburb?

Mountain   many worlds   the
    gods take revenge on their own likeness!

And my grief began with this mountain
which sits above me now like my headstone.

Years will pass. And then   the inscribed
slab will be changed for tombstone and removed.
There will be summerhouses on our mountain.
Soon it will be hemmed in with gardens,

because in outskirts like this they say
the air is better, and it's easier to live:
so it will be cut into plots of land,
and many lines of scaffolding will cross it.

They will straighten my mountain passes.
All my ravines will be upended.
There must be people who want to bring happiness
into their *home*, to have *happiness*.

Happiness at home! Love without fiction.
Imagine: without any stretching of sinews.
I have to be a woman   to endure this!
(There was happiness – when you used to come,

happiness – in my home.) Love without any extra
sweetness given by parting. Or a knife.
Now on the ruins of our happiness
a town will grow: of husbands and wives.

And in that blessed air, while
you can, everyone   should sin –
soon shopkeepers on holidays
will be chewing the cud of their profits,

thinking out new levels and corridors, as
everything leads them back   to their house!
For there has to be someone who needs
a roof with a stork's nest!

Yet under the weight of these foundations
the mountain will not forget   the game.
Though people go astray   they must remember.
And the mountain has   mountains of time.

Obstinate crevices and cracks remain;
in summer homes, they'll realise, too late,
this is no hill, overgrown with families, but
a volcano! Make money out of that!

Can vineyards ever hold the danger
of Vesuvius? A giant without fear cannot
be bound with flax. And the delirium
of lips alone has   the same power:

to make the vineyards stir and turn heavily,
to belch out their lava of hate.
Your daughters shall all become prostitutes
and all your sons turn into   poets!

You shall rear a bastard child, my daughter!
Waste your flesh upon the gypsies, son!
May you never own a piece of fertile land
you   who take your substance from my blood.

Harder than any cornerstone, as
binding as the words of a dying man,
I curse you: do not look for happiness
upon my mountain   where you move like ants!

At some hour unforeseen, some time unknowable,
you will realise, the whole lot of you, how
enormous and without measure is
the mountain of God's seventh law.

Epilogue

There are blanks in memory   cataracts
on our eyes; the seven veils.
I no longer remember you separately
as a face but a white emptiness

without true features. All – is a
whiteness. (My spirit is one
uninterrupted wound.) The chalk of
details must   belong to tailors!

The dome of heaven was   built in a single frame
and oceans   are featureless   a mass of
drops that cannot be distinguished. You
are unique. And love is no detective.

Let now some neighbour say whether your
hair is black or fair, for he can tell.
I leave that to physicians or watchmakers.
What passion has a use for such details?

You are a full, unbroken circle, a
whirlwind or   wholly turned to stone.
I cannot think of you apart from
love. There is an   equals sign.

(In heaps of sleepy down, and falls of
water, hills of foam, there is
a new sound, strange to my hearing,
instead of I   a regal *we*)

and though life's beggared now and
narrowed into   how things are
still I cannot see you joined to
anyone: a
          revenge of memory.

finished 1 December 1924

POEM OF THE END

1

A single post, a point of rusting
   tin in the sky
marks the fated place we
   move to, he and I

on time   as death is
   prompt   strangely
too smooth the gesture of
   his hat to me

menace at the edges of his
   eyes   his mouth tight
shut   strangely too low is the
   bow he makes tonight

on time?   that false note in
   his voice, what
is it the brain alerts to and the
   heart drops at?

under that evil sky, that sign of
   tin and rust,
Six o'clock. There he is waiting
   by the post.

Now we kiss soundlessly, his
   lips stiff as
hands are given to queens, or
   dead people thus

round us the shoving elbows of
   ordinary bustle
and strangely irksome rises the
   screech of a whistle

howls like a dog screaming
    angrier, longer: what
a nightmare strangeness life is
    at death point

and that nightmare reached my waist
    only last night
and now reaches the stars, it has
    grown to its true height

crying silently love love until
    – Has it gone
six, shall we go to the cinema?
    I shout it: home!

2

And what have we come to?
    tents of nomads
thunder and drawn swords over
    our heads, some

terror we expect
    listen   houses
collapsing in the one
    word: home.

It is   the whine of a cossetted
    child lost, it is the
noise a baby makes for
    give and *mine*.

Brother in dissipation, cause
    of this cold fever, you
hurry now to get home just
    as men rush in leaving

like a horse jerking the
   line   rope down in the dust.
Is there even a building there?
   Ten steps before us.

A house on the hill   no higher   a
   house on the top of the hill and
a window under the roof   *is it*
   from the red sun alone

it is burning?   or is it my life
   which must begin again? how
simple poems are: it means I
   must go out into the night
                  and talk to

who shall I tell my sorrow
   my horror greener than ice?
– You've been thinking too much.
   A solemn answer: yes.

3

And the embankment   I hold
   to water   thick and solid as
if we had come to the hanging
   gardens of Semiramis

to water   a strip as colourless
   as a slab for corpses
I am like a female singer holding
   to her music. To this wall.

Blindly   for you won't return
   or listen, even if I bend to
the quencher of all thirst, I am
hanging at the gutter of a roof.

Lunatic. It is not the river
   (I was born naiad) that makes me
shiver now, she was a hand I held
   to, when you walked beside me, a lover

and faithful.
             The dead are faithful
though not to all in their cells; if
   death lies on my left now,
it is at your side I feel it.

Now a shaft of astonishing light, and
   laughter   that cheap tambourine.
– You and I must   have a talk. And
   I shiver: let's be brave, shall we?

4

A blonde mist, a wave of
gauze ruffles, of human
breathing, smoky exhalations
endless talk   the smell of
what? of haste and filth
connivance   shabby acts   all
the secrets of business men
   and ballroom powder.

Family men   like bachelors
move in their rings like middle-aged boys
always joking   always laughing, and
calculating, always calculating
large deals   and little ones, they are
snout-deep in the feathers of some
business arrangement
   and ballroom powder.

(I am half-turned away   is this
our house? I am not mistress here)
Someone   over his cheque book
another bends to a kid glove
a third works at a delicate foot
in patent leather   furtively   the smell
rises of marriage-broking
    and ballroom powder.

In the window is the silver
bite of a tooth: it is the Star of Malta,
which is the sign of stroking, of the love
that leads to pawing and to pinching.
(Yesterday's food perhaps   but
nobody worries if it smells slightly)
    of dirt, commercial tricks
        and ballroom powder.

The chain is too short perhaps even
if it is not steel but platinum?
Look how their three chins shake
like cows munching their own veal
above their sugared necks
the devils swing on a gas lamp
    smelling of business slumps
and another powder
made by Berthold Schwartz
                        genius
intercessor for people:
– You and I must   have a talk
– Let's be brave, shall we?

5

I catch a movement of his
    lips, but he won't
speak – You don't   love me?
    – Yes, but in torment

drained and driven to death
 . (He looks round like an eagle)
– You call this   home? That's
   in the heart. – What *literature*!

Love is flesh, it is a
   flower flooded with blood.
Did you think it was just a
   little chat across a table

a snatched hour and back home again
   the way gentlemen and ladies
play at it? Either love is...
– A shrine?
                          – or else a scar.

A scar   every servant and guest
   can see (and I think silently:
love is a bow-string pulled
   back to the point of breaking).

Love is a bond. That has snapped for
   us   our mouths and lives part
(I begged you not to put a
   spell on me that holy hour

close on mountain heights of
   passion   memory is mist).
Yes, love is a matter of gifts
   thrown in the fire, for nothing

The shellfish crack of his mouth
   is pale, no chance of a smile:
– Love is a large   bed.
   – Or else an empty gulf.

Now his fingers begin to
   beat, no mountains
move. Love is –
                          – *Mine*: yes.
I understand. And so?

The drum beat of his fingers
　　grows (scaffold and square)
– Let's go, he says. For me, let's
　　die, would be easier.

Enough cheap stuff　　rhymes
　　like railway hotel rooms, so:
– love means life　　although
　　the ancients had a different

name.
　　　– Well?
　　　　　　　– A scrap
of handkerchief in a fist
like a fish. – Shall we go? – How,
　　bullet　　rail　　poison

death anyway, choose! I make no
　　plans. A Roman, you
survey the men still alive
　　like an eagle:
　　　　　　　Let's say goodbye.

6

I didn't want this, not
　　this (but listen, quietly,
to want is what bodies do
　　and now we are ghosts only).

And yet I　　didn't say it
　　though the time of the train is set
and the sorrowful honour of leaving
　　is a cup given to women

or perhaps in madness I
　　misheard you　　polite liar:
is this the bouquet that you give your
　　love, this blood-stained honour?

Is it? Sound follows
    sound clearly: was it goodbye
you said? (as sweetly casual
    as a handkerchief dropped without

thought) in this battle
    you are Caesar (What an
insolent thrust, to put the
    weapon of defeat, into my hand

like a trophy). It continues. To
    sound in my ears. As I bow.
– Do you always pretend
    to be forestalled in breaking?

Don't deny this, it
    is a vengeance of Lovelace,
a gesture that does you credit
    while it lifts the flesh

from my bones. Laughter   the laugh of
    death. Moving. Without desire.
That is for others now
    we are shadows to one another.

Hammer the last nail in
    screw up the lead coffin.
– And now a last request.
    – Of course. – Then say nothing

about us   to those who will
    come after me. (The sick
on their stretchers talk of spring.)
– May I ask the same thing?

– Perhaps I should give you a ring?
    – No. Your look is no longer open.
The stamp left on your heart
    would be the ring on your hand.

So now   without any scenes
    I must swallow, silently, furtively.
– A book then? – No, you give those
    to everyone, don't even write them

books…

So now   must   be no
so now   must   be no
must be no crying

In wandering tribes of
fishermen brothers
drink without crying

dance without crying
their blood is hot, they
pay without crying

pearls in a glass
melt, as they run their
world   without crying

Now I am going and this
Harlequin gives his
Pierrette a bone like
a piece of contempt

He throws her the honour
of ending the curtain, the last
word when one inch of lead in
the breast would be hotter and better

Cleaner. My   teeth
press my lips. I can
stop myself crying

pressing the sharpness
into the softest
so without crying

so tribes of nomads
die without crying
burn without crying.

So tribes of fishermen
in ash and song can
hide their dead man.

7

And the embankment. The last one.
   Finished. Separate, and hands apart
like neighbours avoiding one another. We
   walk away from the river, from my

cries. Falling salts of mercury
   I lick off without attention.
No great moon of Solomon
   has been set for my tears in the skies.

A post. Why not beat my forehead to
   blood on it? To smithereens! We are
like fellow criminals, fearing one
   another. (The murdered thing is love.)

Don't say these are lovers? Going into
   the night? Separately? To sleep with others?
– You understand the future is up there?
   he says. And I throw back my head.

To sleep! Like newly-weds over their mat!
　　To sleep! We can't fall into
step. And I plead miserably: take my
　　arm, we aren't convicts to walk like this.

Shock! It's as though his *soul* has touched
　　me　　as his arm leans on mine. The electric
current beats along feverish wiring,
　　and rips. He's leaned on my soul with his arm.

He holds me. Rainbows everywhere. What is more like a
　　rainbow than tears? Rain, a curtain, denser
than beads. I don't know if such embankments can
　　end. But here is a bridge and
　　　　　　　　　　　　　　　　− Well then?

Here? (The hearse is ready.)
　　Peaceful　　his eyes move
upward. − Couldn't you see me home
　　for the very last time?

8

Last　　bridge　　I won't
give up or take out my hand
this is the last bridge
the last bridging between

water　　and firm land:
and I am saving these
coins for death
for Charon, the price of Lethe

this　　shadow money
from my dark hand I press
soundlessly into
the shadowy darkness of his

shadow money it is
no gleam and tinkle in it
coins for shadows:
the dead have enough poppies

This bridge

Lovers for the most
part are without hope: passion
also is just
a bridge, a means of connection

It's warm: to nestle
close at your ribs, to move in
a visionary pause
towards nothing, beside nothing

no   arms no   legs
now, only the bone of my
side is alive where
it presses directly against you

life in that side
only, ear and echo is it: there
I stick like white to
egg yolk, or an eskimo to his fur

adhesive, pressing
joined to you: Siamese
twins are no nearer.
The woman you call mother

when she forgot
all things in motionless triumph
only to carry you:
she did not hold you closer.

Understand: we have
grown into one as we slept and
now I can't jump
because I can't let go your hand

and I won't be torn off
as I press close to you: this
bridge is no husband
but a lover: a just slipping past

our support: for the
river is fed with bodies!
I bite in like a tick
you must tear out my roots to be rid of me

like ivy   like a tick
inhuman   godless
to throw me away like a thing,
when there is

no thing I ever prized
in this empty world of things.
Say this is only a dream,
night still and afterwards morning

an express   to Rome?
Granada? I won't know myself
as I push off
the Himalayas of bedclothes.

But this dark is deep:
now I warm you with my blood, listen
to this flesh.
It is far truer than poems.

If you are warm, who
will you go to tomorrow for that?
This is delirium,
please say this bridge cannot

end
     as it ends.

– Here then? His gesture could
be made by a child, or a god.
– And so? – I am biting in!
For a little more time. The last of it.

9

Blatant as factory buildings,
    as alert to a call
here is the sacred and sublingual
    secret wives keep from husbands and

widows from friends, here is the full
    story that Eve took from the tree:
I am no more than an animal that
    someone has stabbed in the stomach.

Burning. As if the soul had been
    torn away with the skin. Vanished like steam
through a hole is that well-known foolish
    heresy called a soul.

That Christian leprosy:
    steam: save that with your poultices.
There never was such a thing.
    There was a body once, wanted to

live   no longer wants to live.

Forgive me! I didn't mean it!
    The shriek of torn entrails.
So prisoners sentenced to death wait
    for the 4 a.m. firing squad.

At chess perhaps with a grin
    they mock the corridor's eye.
Pawns in the game of chess:
    someone is playing with us.

Who? Kind gods or? Thieves?
    The peephole is filled with an
eye   and the red corridor
    clanks. Listen   the latch lifts.

One drag on tobacco, then
    spit, it's all over, spit,
along this paving of chess squares
    is a direct path   to the ditch

to blood. And the secret eye
    the dormer eye of the moon.

And now, squinting sideways, how
    far away you are already.

10

Closely, like one creature, we
start: there is our café!

There is our island, our shrine, where
in the morning, we people of the

rabble, a couple for a minute only,
conducted a morning service:

with things from country markets, sour
things seen through sleep or   spring.
The coffee was nasty there
entirely made from oats (and

with oats you can extinguish
caprice in fine race-horses).
There was no smell of Araby.
Arcadia was in

that coffee.

But how *she* smiled at us
and sat us down by her,
sad and worldly in her wisdom
a grey-haired paramour.

Her smile was solicitous
(saying: you'll wither! live!),
it was a smile at madness and being
penniless, at yawns   and love

and – this was the chief thing –
at laughter   without reason
smiles   with no deliberation
and our faces   without wrinkles.

Most of all   at youth
at passions   out of this climate
blown in from some other place
flowing from some other source

into that dim café
(burnous and Tunis) where
she smiled at hope and flesh
under old-fashioned clothes.

(My dear friend   I don't complain.
It's just another scar.)
To think how she saw us off,
that proprietress in her cap

stiff   as a Dutch hat...

Not quite remembering, not quite
understanding, we are led away from the festival –
along our street!   no longer ours   that
we walked many times, and no more shall.

Tomorrow the sun will rise in the West.
And then David will break with Jehovah.
– What are we doing? – We are *separating*.
– That's a word that means nothing to me.

It's the most inhumanly senseless
of words: *sep   arating*. (Am I one of a hundred?)
It is simply a word of four syllables and
behind their sound lies: emptiness.

Wait! Is it even correct in Serbian or
Croatian? Is it a Czech whim, this word.
Sep   aration! To *sep   arate!*
It is insane   unnatural

a sound to burst the eardrums, and spread out
far beyond the limits of longing itself.
Separation – the word is not in the Russian
language. Or the language of women. Or men.

Nor in the language of God. What are we – sheep?
To stare about as we eat.
Separation – in what language is it,
when the meaning itself doesn't exist?

or even the sound! Well – an empty one, like
the noise of a saw in your sleep perhaps.
Separation. That belongs to the school of
Khlebnikov's   nightingale-groaning

swan-like…
                    so how does it happen?
Like a lake of water running dry.
Into air. I can feel our hands touching.
To separate. Is a shock of thunder

upon my head – oceans rushing into
a wooden house. This is Oceania's
furthest promontory. And the streets are steep.
To separate. That means to go downward

downhill   the sighing sound of two
heavy soles   and at last a hand receives
the nail in it. A logic that turns
everything over. *To separate*

means we have to become
single creatures   again

we who had grown into one.

11

To lose everything at once –
    what could be tidier?
This is an end to our days
    as we wander in these outskirts,

and to our joys – read burdens –
to our lives, homes and both of us.

Empty dachas. I honour them all,
    as I would an old mother.
To abandon home is action.
    What is empty can't be emptied.

(As for dachas which are part empty,
you may as well burn them right away!)

So – do not flinch! When
    the wound opens.
You must go into the outskirts
    and simply rip out the stitches.

Let me put this plainly: love
is no more than a line of stitches,

a seam, yes, which is no protection.
    So don't beg to be shielded.
These stitches hold the dead to the earth.
    that is how we are stitched

and time will show what kind of
stitching: single – or reinforced.

Whichever, rip the stitches out,
    friend, leave only shreds.
I'm glad they tear out easily –
    better to rip than unravel.

Look under the basting – there:
a living red vein not decay.

Rip and tear, you lose nothing.
    Let's make for the outskirts
Let's go way out of town!
    And divorce our spirits for ever.

There's a wind in the brain, today:
an execution to witness.

The one who leaves feels no loss
    even as dawn is breaking.
I sewed your whole life in a night
    perfectly, without basting.

If it's crooked, don't complain!
– You can just rip out the stitches.

Ours are untidy souls. Both
    are covered with scars.
Let's make a violent sweep of this:
    in the outskirts, out of time.

To the suburbs! The heel of fate
    is pressed into wet clay –
So blame my hurried work
    friend, or the living thread

which clings, however tangled.
Here is the last street lamp.

★

– Here then? A glance, as if in
conspiracy. A glance. From a lesser race.
A glance – Can we climb the mountain,
for the very last time?

12

Dense as a horse mane is:
    rain in our eyes. And hills.
We have passed the suburb.
    Now we are out of town,

which is there   but not for us.
    Stepmother   not mother.
Nowhere   is lying ahead.
    And here   is where we fall.

A field with. A fence and.
    Brother and sister. Standing.
Life is   only a suburb:
    so you must build elsewhere.

Ugh, what a lost cause
    it is, ladies and gentlemen,
for the whole world is   suburb:
    Where   are the real towns?

Rain rips at us madly.
    We stand and break with each other.
In three months, these must be
    the first moments of sharing.

Is it true, God, that you even
    tried to borrow from Job?
Well, it didn't come off.
    Still. We are. Outside town.

Beyond it! Understand? Outside!
    That means   we've passed the walls.
Life is a place where it's forbidden
    to live. Like the Hebrew quarter.

And isn't it more worthy to
    become an eternal Jew?
Anyone not   a reptile
    suffers the same pogrom.

Life is for converts only
    Judases of all faiths.
Let's go to leprous islands
    or hell   anywhere   only not

life   which puts up with traitors, with
    those who are sheep   to butchers!
This paper which gives me the
    right to live – I stamp. With my feet.

Stamp! for the shield of David.
    Vengeance! for heaps of bodies
and they say after all (delicious) the
    Jews didn't want to live!

Ghetto of the chosen. Beyond this
    ditch. No mercy
In this   most Christian of worlds
    all poets   are Jews.

13

This is how they sharpen knives on a
    stone, and sweep sawdust up with
brooms. Under my hands there is
    something wet and furry.

Now where are those twin male
    virtues: strength, dryness?
Here beneath my hand I can
    feel   tears. Not rain!

What temptations can still be
    spoken of? Property is   water.
Since I felt your diamond eyes under
    my hands, flowing.

There is no more I can lose. We have
    reached the end of ending.
And so I simply stroke, and
    stroke. And stroke your face.

This is the kind of pride we have:
    Marinkas   are Polish girls.
Since now the eyes of an eagle weep
    underneath these hands...

Can you be crying? My friend, my
    – everything! Please forgive me!
How large and salty now is the
    taste of this in my fist.

Male tears are – cruel! They
    rise over my head! Weep,
there will soon be others to
    heal any guilt towards me.

Fish of   identic-
    al sea. A sweep upward! like
... any dead shells and any
    lips upon lips.

In tears.
Wormwood
to taste.
– And tomorrow
when
I am awake?

14

A slope like a path   for
sheep. With town noises.
Three trollops approach.
They are laughing. At tears.

They are laughing   the full noon of
their bellies shake, like waves!
They laugh at the
                         inappropriate
disgraceful, male

tears of yours, visible
through the rain   like scars!
Like a shameful   pearl on
the bronze of a warrior.

These first and last tears
pour them now – for me –
for your tears   are pearls
that I wear in my crown.

And my eyes are not lowered.
I stare through   the shower.
Yes, dolls of Venus
stare at me! because

this is a closer bond
than the transport of lying down.
The Song of Songs itself
gives place to our speech,

infamous birds as we are
Solomon bows to us, for
our simultaneous cries
are   something more than a dream!

And into the hollow waves of
darkness – hunched and level –
without trace – in silence –
something sinks like a ship.

1924

An Attempt at Jealousy

How is your life with the other one,
    simpler, isn't it? One   stroke of the oar
then a long coastline, and soon
    even the memory of me

will be a floating island
    (in the sky, not on the waters):
spirits, spirits, you will be
    sisters, and never lovers.

How is your life with an ordinary
    woman?   without godhead?
Now that your sovereign has
    been deposed (and you have stepped down).

How is your life? Are you fussing?
    flinching? How   do you get up?
The tax of deathless vulgarity
    can you cope with it, poor man?

'Scenes and hysterics   I've had
    enough! I'll rent my own house.'
How is your life with the other one
    now, you that I chose for my own?

More to your taste, more delicious
    is it, your food? Don't moan if you sicken.
How is your life with an *image*
    you, who walked on Sinai?

How is your life with a stranger
    from this world? Can you (be frank)
love her? Or do you   feel shame
    like Zeus' reins on your forehead?

How is your life? Are you
    healthy? How do you   sing?
How do you deal with the pain
    of an undying conscience, poor man?

How is your life with a piece of market
    stuff, at a steep price.
After Carrara marble,
    how is your life with the dust of

plaster now? (God was hewn from
    stone, but he is smashed to bits.)
How do you live with one of a
    thousand women   after Lilith?

Sated with newness, are you?
    Now you are grown cold to magic,
how is your life with an
    earthly woman, without a sixth

sense? Tell me: are you happy?
    Not? In a shallow pit? How is
your life, my love? Is it as
    hard as mine with another man?

1924

To Boris Pasternak

Distance: versts, miles…
divide us; they've dispersed us,
to make us behave quietly
at our different ends of the earth.

Distance: how many miles of it
lie between us now – disconnected –
crucified – then dissected.
And they don't know – it unites us.

Our spirits and sinews fuse,
there's no discord between us.
though our separated pieces
                         lie outside
the moat – for eagles!

This conspiracy of miles
has not yet disconcerted us,
however much they've pushed us, like
orphans into backwaters.

– What then? Well. Now it's March!
And we're scattered like some pack of cards!

1925

New Year's Greetings

i.m. Rainer Maria Rilke

Happy New Year – new sphere – horizon – haven!
This is my first letter to your new address,
– notorious region, misunderstood, unsettled –,
as clamorous and empty as the Aeolian tower;
my very first letter to you from the yesterday
in which I suddenly found myself without you,
my own homeland become one of the stars...
Shall I tell you how I heard the news?
No earthquake or avalanche announced it,
only someone – might have been anyone – said
he'd read it in a daily paper. 'Show me the article –
where did it happen?' 'The mountains.
(*I think of pine branches in a window*)
Don't you ever *read* newspapers?'
'The article?' 'I don't have it with me.'
'*Where* did it happen?' 'In a sanatorium.'
(*A rented paradise.*) 'Please tell me when.'
'Yesterday, or the day before, I can't remember.
Will you write something for us?' 'No, I won't.
He's family. *I'm not treacherous.*'

Happy New Year, then, which begins tomorrow!
Shall I tell you what I did when I heard
of your – no, that's a slip of the tongue.
I don't use silly words like Life and Death –
So tell me, Rainer, how was your ride?
How was it when your heart burst open?
Was it like riding Orlov's horses – wild
and fast as eagles fly – as you once told me?
Did it take your breath away? Was it more intense –
sweeter? Russian eagles have a blood tie
with the other world, and in Russia
you see the other world in this.

It belongs to us, that long night of stars
I speak of with a secret smile...

You timed your crossing well.
                              Dear friend,
if Russian script replaces German letters here
it's not because the dead have to put up with
everything, as a beggar does, – it's because
the world you live in now is *ours*.
– I knew as much when I was thirteen...

Am I digressing? No, that isn't possible.
Nothing can distract my thoughts from you.
Every one of them, *du Lieber*, every syllable
leads me towards you in whatever language.
German is as native to me as Russian,
and most of all the language Angels speak.
There is no place where you are not.
Except the grave...

Do you ever – think about me, I wonder?
What do you feel now, what is it like up there?
How was your first sight of the Universe,
a last vision of the whole planet –
which must include this poet remaining in it,
not yet ashes, still a spirit in a body –
seen from however many miles stretch
from Creation to eternity, far above
the Mediterranean in its crystal saucer –
where else would you look, leaning out
with your elbows on the edge of your box seat
if not on this poet, with her many griefs...

I live in Bellevue: these suburban outskirts,
have birds' nests in the branches. Glance
at your tour guide: Bellevue is a fortress
with a good view of Paris and its palaces.
How absurd we must seem as you lean out
on the crimson velvet edge of your theatre box,

looking down from an infinite height
on our Bellevue and Belvederes!
Skip the details. Here's an urgent fact.
The New Year is already on my door step.
With whom can I clink a glass across
the table tonight? And with what?
Cotton wool? I have no champagne froth.
The New Year is striking. Why am I here?
What is there to do in this New Year?
If such an orb of light as you can go out
then neither life nor death has any meaning.

I shall only understand when we meet again.
What joy to end with you, begin with you.
Let us clink across the table, not with pub
glasses, but as if our souls fused.
I look upon your cross. Everywhere
outside time and place belongs to us.
Leaves and conifers. Months and weeks
in rainy city fringes without people!
And mornings – all of them spent together.
Of course I see poorly down here in a pit
Of course you see better from up there.

Nothing turned out between us. That is the truth:
Nothing happened. *Nothing.*

We know our roles, and both are large enough
not to mention that. Don't wait
for the one who stands out from the crowd
– or the one who stands inside it either.
                              An eternal tune:
don't speak of the one on death row
cut from the same cloth and remembered
by the same mouth. Only one world
was ours, and that was where we shone;
exchanging everything else to do so.

So, from these outskirts: Happy new world,
Rainer! Happy new sounds!
Everything once seemed to stand in your way,
even passion and friendship. No longer.
Happy new echoes, Rainer!

I used to dream at my school desk about rivers
and mountains. How is your landscape without tourists?
Was I right, Rainer, to think of heaven as stormy
and mountainous – not the way widows imagine?
And not just one heaven, but another over it?
With terraces? Something like the Tatra?
Heaven must resemble an amphitheatre.
Was I right to think of God as a Baobab?
Is there only one God – or another over Him?

I know wherever you are, there are poems.
How do you write without a table for your elbow,
or even a forehead for your cupped hand?
Drop me a line in your usual scrawl!
Death must offer many occasions for poetry.
Are you pleased, Rainer, with your new verse?
I can't go any further, now I've learned
a language with so many new meanings.
Goodbye. Until we meet each other
– if we do – face to face. Look
at the whole earth and the oceans, Rainer.
Look at all of me.

If you can, drop me a scribbled line
– Happy new writing, Rainer – and
I'll climb a staircase bearing gifts to you
hoping to feel your hand on my head,
I'll carry my New Year's glass, without spilling
a tear-drop, over the Rhone and Rarogne
– your resting place – which marks our final parting.

Put this into the hands of Rainer – Maria – Rilke!

from *THE RATCATCHER*

from *Chapter 1*

Hamelin, the good-mannered
  town of window-boxes,
well-stocked with
  warehouses
         Paradise Town!

How God must love
  these sensible
townspeople. Every one
  is righteous:

Goody-goody, always-right, always-provided-for,
stocked-up-in-time. It's Paradise Town!

Here are no riddles.
  All is smooth and peaceable.
Only good habits in
        Paradise
        Town.

In God's sweet
  backwater
(The Devil turns his
  nose up here):

It's goody-goody Paradise (owned by Schmidt and Mayers).
A town for an Emperor. Give way to your elders!

Everywhere is tranquil.
  No fire. The whole place
must belong to Abel.
  Isn't that
        Paradise?

Those who are not
    too cold or too hot
travel straight to Hamelin
    straight into Hamelin:

Lullaby and ermine-down, this is Paradise Town!
Everywhere is good advice and go-to-sleep on time Town!
First watch!
First watch!
With the world all contact's lost!
Is the dog out? And the cat in?
Did you hear the early warning.

Take your servants out of harness
    Shake your pipe – you've time for that –
but leave your workbench now because
    'Morgen ist auch ein tag'

Ten to ten!
Ten to ten.
Put your woolly earplugs in.
In the desk with all your schoolbooks
Set your clocks to ring at five.

Shopkeeper, leave your chalk,
    Housewife, your mending.
Look to your feather bed:
    'Morgen ist auch ein tag'

Ten o'clock.
Ten o'clock
No more interruptions.
Keys turned? Bolts drawn?
That was the third call.

Cl-o-ose your Bible, Dad.
Housewife, put your bonnet on.
Hus-band, your nightcap.
'Morgen ist…'

    All asleep.
That's the Hameliners!

from *Chapter 2*

Dreams

In all other cities,
   in mine, for instance, (out of bounds)
husbands see mermaids, and
   wives dream of Byrons.

Children see devils,
   and servants see horsemen.
But what can these, Morpheus,
   citizens so sinless

dream of at night – Say *what*?
   They don't need to think hard.
The husband sees – his wife!
   The wife sees her husband!

The baby sees a teat.
   And that beauty, fat of cheek,
sees a sock of her father's
   that she's been darning.

The Cook tries the food out.
   The 'Ober' gives his orders.
It's all as it ought to be,
   all as it ought to be.

As stitches go smoothly
　　along a knitting needle
Peter sees Paul (what else?).
　　And Paul sees Peter.

A grandfather dreams of
　　grandchildren.
Journalists – of some full-stop!
　　The maid – a kind master.

Commandments for Kaspar.
　　A sermon for the Pastor.
To sleep has its uses,
　　it isn't really wasteful!

The sausage-maker dreams of
　　poods of fat sausages;
a judge of a pair of scales
　　(like the apothecary).

Teachers dream of canes.
　　A tailor of goods for sale.
And a dog of his bone?
　　Wrong! He sees his collar!

The Cook sees a plucked bird.
　　The laundress sees velveteen.
Just as it's been laid down
　　in the prescription.

And what of the Bürgermeister?
　　Sleep is like waking
once you are Bürgermeister
　　what else can you dream about?

Except looking over
　　the citizens who serve you.
That's what the Bürgermeister
　　sees: all his servants!

That's how things have to be!
   That's how they are arranged!
That's the prescription!
   That's the prescription!

(My tone may be playful – yes,
   the old has some virtue)
So let us not use up
   our rhymes over nothing.

As the Bürgermeister sleeps, let's
   slip into his room (Tsar
of Works and Constructions!)
   How solidly the building stands...

It's worth our attention.

from *The Children's Paradise*

To live means – ageing,
turning grey relentlessly.
To live is – for those you hate!
Life has no eternal things.

In my kingdom: no butchers, no jails.
   Only ice there! Only blue there!
Under the roof of shivering waters
   pearls the size of walnuts

girls wear and boys hunt.
There's – a bath – for everyone.

Pearls are a wondrous illness.
Fall asleep then. Sleep. And vanish.

Dry twigs are grey. Do you want
scarlet? – Try my coral branch!

In my kingdom: no mumps; no measles,
   medieval history, serious matters,
no execution of Jan Hus. No discrimination.
   No more need for childish terrors.

Only blue. And lovely summer.
Time – for all things – without measure.

Softly, softly, children. You're
going to a quiet school – under the water.

Run with your rosy cheeks
into the eternal streams.

Someone: Chalk. Someone: Slime.
Someone calling: Got my feet wet.

Someone: Surge. Someone: Rumble.
Someone: Got a gulp of lake!

2

Diving boys and swimming girls
Look, the water's on their fingers.

Pearls are scattered for them!
The water's at their ankles,

sneaking up their little knees. They cry:
– Chrys – o – lite.

Red moss! Blue caves!
(Feet go deeper. Skies rise higher.)

Mirror boxes. Crystal balls. Something's
been left behind, something grows closer…

You're stuck up to the knees! Careful.
– Ah this chrys-o-prase!

The water is shoulder high on
little mice in schoolday clothes.

Little snub-nose, – higher, higher
now the water's at your throat.

It's sweeter than bed linen...
– Crystals! Crystals!

In my kingdom: (The flute sounds the gentlest *dolce*)
    Time dwindles, eyes grow larger.
Is that a sea gull? or is it a baby's bonnet?
    Legs grow heavy, hearts grow lighter.

Water reaches to the chin.
Mourn, friends and relatives!

Isn't this a fine palace
for the Bürgermeister's daughter?

Here are eternal dreams, words without pathways.
    The flute grows sweeter, hearts more quiet.
Follow without thinking. Listen. No need for thought!
    The flute becomes sweeter still, hearts even quieter.

– *Mutter.* Don't call me in for supper...
                                            Bu-u-bbles!

1925

from *POEMS TO A SON*

Forget us, children. Our conscience
   need not belong to you.
You can be free to write the tale
   of your own days and passions.

Here in this family album
   lies the salt family of Lot.
It is for you to reckon up
   the many claims on Sodom.

You didn't fight your brothers
   my curly headed boy!
So this is your time, this is your day.
   The land is purely yours.

Sin, cross, quarrel, anger,
   these are ours. There have been
too many funerals held by now
   for an Eden you've never seen

whose fruit you never tasted.
   So now, put off your mourning.
Understand: they are blind
   who lead you, but then

our quarrel is not your quarrel,
   So as you rush from Meudon
and race to the Kuban
   children, prepare for battle

in the field of your own days.

January 1932

Homesickness

Homesickness! that long
exposed weariness!
It's all the same to me now
where I am   altogether lonely

or what stones I wander over
home with a shopping bag to
a house that is no more mine
than a hospital or a barracks.

It's all the same to me, captive
lion   what faces I move through
bristling, or what human crowd will
cast me out   as it must

into myself, into my separate internal
world, a Kamchatka bear without ice.
Where I fail to fit in (and I'm not trying) or
where I'm humiliated   it's all the same.

And I won't be seduced by the thought of
my native language, its milky call.
How can it matter   in what tongue I
am misunderstood by whoever I meet

(or by what readers, swallowing
newsprint, squeezing for gossip?)
They all belong to the twentieth
century, and   I am before time,

stunned, like a log left
behind from an avenue of trees.
People are all the same to me, everything
is the same, and it may be the most

indifferent of all   are these
signs and tokens which once were
native   but the dates have been
rubbed out: the soul was born somewhere.

For my country has taken so little care
of me that even the sharpest spy could
go over my whole spirit and would
detect no native stain there.

Houses are alien, churches are empty
everything   is the same:
But if by the side of the path one
particular bush rises
                    the rowanberry...

                                    1934

I opened my veins

I opened my veins.   Unstoppably
life spurts out with no remedy.
Now I set out bowls and plates.
Every bowl will be shallow.
Every plate will be small.
          And overflowing their rims,
into the black earth, to nourish
the rushes unstoppably
without cure, gushes
poetry...

1934

Epitaph

1

Just going out for a minute –
left your work (which the idle
call chaos) behind on the table.
And left the chair behind when   you went where?

I ask around all Paris, for it's
only in stories or pictures
that people rise to the skies:
where is your soul gone, where?

In the cupboard, two-doored like a shrine,
look   all your books are in place.
In each line the letters are there.
Where has it gone to, your face?

Your face
your warmth
your shoulder

where did they go?

2

Useless with eyes   like nails to
penetrate the black soil
As true   as a nail in the mind
you are not here, not here.

It's useless   turning my eyes
and fumbling round the whole sky.
Rain. Pails of rain-water. But
you are not there, not there.

Neither one of the two. Bone is
too much bone. And spirit is too much spirit.
Where is the real you? All of you?
Too much here. Too much there.

And I won't exchange you for sand
and steam. You took me for kin,
and I won't give you up for a corpse
and a ghost: a here, and a there.

It's not you, not you, not you,
however much priests intone
that death and life are one:
God's too much God, worm – too much worm!

You are one thing, corpse and spirit.
We won't give you up for the smoke of
censers
or flowers
on graves

If you *are* anywhere, it's here in
us: and we honour best all those who
have gone by despising division.
It is all of you   that has gone.

3

Because once when you were young and bold
you did not leave me to rot alive among
bodies without souls or fall dead among walls
I will not let you   die altogether.

Because, fresh and clean, you took me
out by the hand, to freedom   and brought spring leaves
in bundles into my house   I shall not
let you be grown over with weeds and forgotten.

And because you met the status of my
first grey hairs like a son   with pride
greeting their terror with a child's joy:
I shall not let you go grey into men's hearts.

4

The blow   muffled through years of
    forgetting, of not knowing:
That blow reaches me now like the song of a
    woman, or like horses neighing.

Through an inert building, a song of passion and
    the blow comes:
dulled by forgetfulness, by not knowing which is
    a soundless thicket.

It is the sin of memory, which has no eyes or
    lips or flesh or nose,
the silt of all the days and nights
    we have been without each other

the blow is muffled with moss and waterweed:
    so ivy devours the
core of the living thing it is ruining
    – a knife through a feather bed.

Window wadding, our ears are plugged with it
    and with that other wool
outside windows of snow and the weight of spiritless
    years: and the blow is muffled.

1935

Readers of Newspapers

It crawls, the underground snake,
crawls, with its load of people.
And each one   has his
newspaper, his skin
disease; a twitch of chewing;
newspaper *caries*.
Masticators of gum,
readers of newspapers.

And who are the readers? old men? athletes?
soldiers? No face, no features,
no age. Skeletons – there's no
face, only the newspaper page.

All Paris   is dressed
this way from forehead to navel.
Give it up, girl, or
you'll give birth to
a reader of newspapers.

Sway   he lived with his sister.
Swaying   he killed his father.
They blow themselves up with pettiness
as if they were swaying with drink.

For such gentlemen   what
is the sunset or the sunrise?
They swallow emptiness,
these readers of newspapers.

For news   read: calumnies.
For news   read: embezzling,
in every column   slander
every paragraph some   disgusting thing.

With what, at the Last Judgement
will you come before the light?
Grabbers of small moments,
readers of newspapers.

Gone! Lost! Vanished! So,
the old maternal terror.
But mother, the Gutenberg Press
is more terrible than Schwarz' powder.

It's better to go to a graveyard
than into the   prurient
sickbay of scab-scratchers,
these readers of newspapers.

And who is it rots our sons
now in the prime of their life?
Those corrupters of blood
the *writers* of newspapers.

Look, friends   much
stronger than in these lines, do
I think this, when with
a manuscript in my hand

I stand before the face
there is no   emptier place
than before the absent
face of an editor
of newspapers' evil filth.

1935

Desk

1

My desk, most loyal friend
    thank you. You've been with me on
every road I've taken.
    My scar and my protection.

My loaded writing mule.
    Your tough legs have endured
the weight of all my dreams, and
    burdens of piled-up thoughts.

Thank you   for toughening me.
    No worldly joy could pass
your severe looking-glass
    you blocked the first temptation,

and every base desire
    your heavy oak outweighed
lions of hate, elephants
    of spite   you intercepted.

Thank you for growing with me
    as my need grew in size
I've been laid out across you
    so many years   alive

while you've grown broad and wide
    and overcome me.   Yes,
however my mouth opens
    you stretch out   limitless.

You've nailed me to your wood.
    I'm glad.   To be pursued.
And torn up.   At first light.
    To be caught.   And commanded:

Fugitive. Back to your chair!
   I'm glad you've guarded me
and bent my life away
   from blessings that don't last,

as wizards guide sleep walkers!
   My battles burn as signs.
You even use my blood to set out
   all my acts in lines –

in columns, as you are a pillar
   of light. My source of power!
You lead me as the Hebrews once
   were led forward by fire.

Take blessings now from me,
   as one put to the test, on
elbows, forehead, knotted knees,
   your knife edge   to my breast.

2

I celebrate thirty years
   of union   truer than love
I know every notch in your wood.
You know the lines in my face.

Haven't you written them there?
   devouring reams of paper
denying me any tomorrow
   teaching me only today.

You've thrown my important letters
   and money   in floods together,
repeating: for every single verse
   today has to be the deadline.

You've warned me of retribution
   not to be measured in spoonfulls.
And when   my body will be laid out,
   great fool! Let it be on you then.

3

The rest of you can eat me up
   I just record your behaviour!
For you they'll find dining tables
   to lay you out.   This desk for me!

Because I've been happy with little
   there are foods I've never tasted.
The rest of you dine slowly.
   You've eaten too much and too often.

Places are already chosen
   long before birth for everyone.
The place of adventures is settled,
   and the places of gratification.

Truffles for you not pencils.
   Pickles instead of dactyls
and you express your pleasure
   in belches and not in verses.

At your head funeral candles
   must be thick-legged asparagus:
surely your road from this world
   will cross a dessert table!

Let's puff Havana tobacco
   on either side of you then;
and let your shrouds be made
   from the finest of Dutch linen.

And so as not to waste such
   fine cloth let them shake you
with left-overs and crumbs
   into the grave that waits for you.

Your souls at the   post mortem
   will be like stuffed capons.
But I shall be there naked
   with only two wings for cover.

1933-5

Bus

The bus jumped, like a brazen
evil spirit,   a demon
cutting across the traffic
in streets as cramped as footnotes,
it rushed on its way   shaking
like a concert-hall vibrating
with applause.   And we shook in it!
Demons too.   Have you seen
seeds under a tap? We were
like peas in boiling soup,
or Easter toys dancing in
alcohol.   Mortared grain!
Teeth in a chilled mouth.

What   has been shaken out   someone
could use for a chandelier:
all the beads   and the bones
of an old woman. A necklace
on that girl's breast. Bouncing.
The child at his mother's nipple.
Shaken without reference
like pears   all of us   shaken
in *vibrato*, like violins.
The violence shook our souls
into laughter, and back into childhood.

Young again. Yes. The joy of that
being thrown into girlhood! Or
perhaps further back, to become
a tomboy with toothy grin.
        It was as if the piper
        had led us, not out of town, but
        right out of the calendar.

Laughter exhausted us all.
I was too weak to stand.
Enfeebled, I kept on my feet only
by holding your belt in my hand.

Askew, head on, the bus was
crazed like a bull, it leapt
as if at a red cloth,
to rush round a sharp bend
and then, quite suddenly
stopped.
   … So, between hills, the creature
   lay obedient and still.
   Lord, what blue surrounded us,
   how everywhere was green!

The hurt of living gone,
like January's tin.
Green was everywhere,
a strange and tender green.

A moist, uneasy noise of green
flowed through our veins' gutters.
Green struck my head open,
and freed me from all thinking!

A moist, wood-twig smoke of green
flowed through our veins' gutters.
Green struck my head open.
It overflowed me completely!

Inside me, warmth and birdsong.
You could drink both of them from
the two halves of my skull —
(Slavs did that with enemies).

Green rose, green shoots, green
fused to a single emerald.
The green smell of the earth had
struck deeply. (No buffalo feels that.)

Malachite. Sapphire. Unneeded.
The eye and ear restored –
Falcons don't see tillage,
prisoners don't hear birds.

My eye is ripe with green.
Now I see no misfortune
(or madness – it was true reason!)
to leave a throne and fall

on all fours like a beast
and dig his nose in the grass...
He wasn't mad, that sovereign
Nebuchadnezzar, munching

stalks of grass – but a Tsar,
a herbivorous, cereal-loving
brother of Jean-Jacques Rousseau...
This green of the earth has given
my legs the power to run

into heaven.
I've taken in so much
green juice and energy I am
as powerful as a hero.
The green of the earth has struck
my cheeks. And there it glows.

For an hour, under cherry trees,
God allowed me to think
that my own, my old, face
could be the same colour as these.

Young people may laugh. Perhaps
I'd be better off standing under
some old tower, than mistaking
that cherry-tree colour
for the colour of my

face…

With grey hair like mine? But then,
apple blossom is grey. And God has brought me close
to everyone of his creatures
I am *closer*   as well as *lower*…

a sister to all creation
from the buttercup to the mare –
So I blew in my hands, like a trumpet.
I even dared to leap!

As old people rejoice
without shame on a roundabout,
I believed my hair was brown
again, no grey streak in it.

So, with my branch of green
I could drive my friend like a goose,
and watch his sail-cloth suit
turn into true sails –

Surely my soul was prepared
to sail beyond the ocean.
(The earth had been a seabed –
it laughed now with vegetation.)

My companion was only slender
    in the waist.   His heart was thick.
(How his white canvas puckered,
    and came to rest in the green.)

Faith. Aurora. Soul's blue.
    Never dilute or measured.
Idiot soul!   And yet Peru
    will yield to the madness of it!

My friend became heavy to lead,
    as a child does for no reason,
(I found my own bold web
    as lovely as any spider's).

Suddenly   like a vast frame
for a living miracle: Gates!
Between their marble, I could
stand, like an ancient sign,

uniting myself and the landscape;
a frame in which I remain,
between gates that lead to no castle,
gates that lead to no farmhouse,

gates   like a lion's jaws
which let in light. Gates
leading to where? Into
happiness   came the answer,

twofold...

Happiness? Far away.   North of here.
Somewhere else. Some other time.
Happiness? Even the scent is cold.
I looked for it once, on all fours.

When I was four years old, looking
for a clover with four leaves.
What do these numbers matter?
Happiness? Cows feed on it.

The young are in ruminant company
of two jaws and four hooves.
Happiness stamps its feet.
It doesn't stand looking at gates.

The wood block and the well.
Remember that old tale?
Of cold water streaming past
an open, longing mouth,

and the water missing the mouth
as if in a strange dream.
There's never enough water,
(the sea's not enough for me).

From opened veins, water
flows on to moist earth –
Water keeps passing by
as life does, in a dream.

And now I've wiped my cheeks
I know the exact force
of the streams that miss my hands
and pass my thirsting

mouth

The tree, in its cloud of blossom,
was a dream avalanche over us.
With a smile, my companion compared it
to a 'cauliflower in white sauce'.

That phrase struck into my heart, loud
as thunder. Now grant me encounters
with thieves and pillagers, Lord, rather
than bed in the hay with a *gourmand*!

A thief can rob – and not touch your face.
You'll be fleeced, but your soul will escape.
But a *gourmand* must finger and pinch, before
he puts you aside, to eat later.

I can throw off my rings. Or my fingers.
You can strip my hide, and wear it.
But a *gourmand* demands the brain and heart
to the last groan of their torment.

The thief will go off. In his pockets
my jewels, the cross from my breast.
A toothbrush ends all romance
with *gourmands*.
               Don't fall in their hands!

And you, who could be loved royally
as an evergreen, shall be
as nameless as cauliflower in my mouth:
I take this revenge – for the tree!

1934-6

When I look at the flight of the leaves

When I look at the flight of the leaves in
   their floating down on to the paving of cobbles
and see them swept up as if by an
   artist who has finished his picture at last

I think how (already nobody likes either
   the way I stand, or my thoughtful face)
a manifestly yellow, decidedly
   rusty leaf – has been left behind on the tree.

1936

from *POEMS TO CZECHOSLOVAKIA*

6

They took   quickly, they took   hugely,
  took the mountains and their entrails.
They took our coal, and took our steel
  from us, lead they took also and crystal.

They took the sugar, and they took the clover
  they took the North and took the West.
They took the hive, and took the haystack
  they took the South from us, and took the East.

Vary   they took and Tatras   they took,
  they took the near at hand and far away.
But   worse than taking paradise on earth from us
  they won the battle for our native land.

Bullets they took from us, they took our rifles
  minerals they took, and comrades too.
But while our mouths have spittle in them
  the whole country   is still armed.

8

What tears in eyes now
weeping with anger and love
Czechoslovakia's tears
Spain in its own blood

and what a black mountain
has blocked the world   from the light.
It's time – It's time – It's time
to give back to God   his ticket.

I refuse to be. In
the madhouse of the inhuman
I refuse   to live.
With the wolves of the market place

I refuse   to howl.
Among the sharks of the plain
I refuse to swim   down
where moving backs make a current.

I have no need of holes
for ears, nor prophetic eyes:
to your mad world there is
one answer: to refuse!

1938

Notes

Girlfriend

p. 4   Sophia Yakovlevna Parnok (originally Parnokh; 1885-1933) was a poet, dramatist, librettist and a translator of Baudelaire. She was born into a Jewish pharmacist's family in Taganrog on the Black Sea coast of Russia. She studied in Geneva, where she lived for a time, and thereafter moved between St Petersburg and Moscow. Her brother Valentin Parnokh was also a well-known poet. Sophia married Vladimir Volkenstein in June 1906; they were divorced in 1909. She was seven years older than Tsvetaeva when they began their love affair in 1914. Parnok's first book of poems spoke openly of lesbian desire. By 1928 Soviet censorship decided her poetry was unlawful, and from then until her death she was unable to publish.

We are keeping an eye on the girls

p. 23   *kvass*: a common Russian drink, non-alcoholic, made from fermented rye bread. Razin: Stenka Razin was a Cossack leader of the seventeenth-century peasant rebellion in Russia. According to legend, he sacrificed a Persian girl whom he loved to the river Volga.

No one has taken anything away

p. 24   This poem is addressed to Osip Mandelstam (1892–1938); he and Tsvetaeva were lovers for a short while in 1916.
Derzhavin: (1743–1816) the most important Russian poet writing before Pushkin.

You throw back your head

p. 25   Also written for Mandelstam, who recorded a similar excitement in walking about Moscow in his own poem 'With no confidence in miracles of redemption' (*Tristia*, 1922).

Where does this tenderness come from?

p. 26   Again addressed to Mandelstam.

Today or tomorrow the snow will melt

p. 28   Rogozhin: character in Dostoyevsky's novel *The Idiot*, who sets out to kill Prince Myshkin.

Verses about Moscow

p. 29   I lift you up: the first lyric from this cycle is addressed to Tsvetaeva's
daughter, Alya.

forty times forty [churches]: a phrase often used of Moscow.

Vagankovo: well-known cemetery in Moscow, where Tsvetaeva's
parents were buried.

p. 30   Strange and beautiful brother: the second lyric is addressed to
Mandelstam, who lived in St Petersburg, and to whom Tsvetaeva offers
her native city, Moscow.

Spassky gate/five cathedrals: in the Kremlin.

Inadvertent Joy: a wonder-working icon of the Virgin Mary, not far
from the Kremlin.

Peter: Peter the Great (1689–1725) founded St Petersburg, which
replaced Moscow as his capital.

p. 32   Child Panteleimon: a saint revered in the Orthodox Church,
supposed to protect people's health.

Iversky heart: another wonder-working icon of the Virgin Mary, for
which a special chapel was built, and which was taken to the city of
Vladimir in 1812.

Poems for Akhmatova

p. 38   Anna Akhmatova (1889–1966).

Ah!: in Russian '*akh*', the first syllable of the poet's name.

p. 39   Tsarskoselsky: Akhmatova spent much of her youth in, and there-
after frequently revisited, the imperial town of Tsarskoe Selo, near St
Petersburg.

Poems for Blok

p. 41   Alexander Blok (1880–1921), Symbolist poet, with whom
Tsvetaeva was never personally acquainted, although she met him
briefly on two occasions.

five signs: in the old orthography (altered after the Revolution, but
always appealing to Tsvetaeva) Blok's name was spelt with five letters
– these four, plus a 'hard sign'.

spectre/knight/snow/wind: examples of images that deliberately recall
images and words from poems by Blok himself.

p. 43   Poem 3: the first two lines and the penultimate line of this poem
are a rephrasing of words from a well-known prayer sung in the
Orthodox Church.

your river Neva: Blok's native city was St Petersburg. The first phrase
of this poem '*U menya v Moskve*' could also be translated, to emphasise
the contrast, 'In my Moscow'.

red calico of Kaluga: literally, 'Kaluga native calico'. Tsvetaeva evokes a typical peasant scene at Tarusa, in Kaluga, where she spent her childhood summers in the family dacha.

p. 45 Poem 9 is dated 9 May 1920, and Tsvetaeva notes on her manuscript: 'On the day when the powder cellars were blown up in the Khodynka and the window panes were shattered in the Polytechnic Museum, where Blok was reading.'

blue cloak: an image from Blok's poem 'O podvigakh, o doblesty-akh, o slave', written in 1908 and addressed to his wife.

We shall call for the sun...: referring to Blok's poem 'Golos iz khora' (1910), with its lines: 'You will call for the sun's rising —/the sun will lie low' (in the version by Jon Stallworthy and Peter France, in Alexander Blok, Selected Poems, Manchester, Carcanet 2000).

Swans' Encampment

p. 49 This is one lyric from a long cycle of poems written in Moscow between 1917–21, which was never published in Tsvetaeva's lifetime. In many of them she adapts the lay of Prince Igor, and the tone of a lamenting Yaroslavna, to describe the heroic nobility of the White Army's self-sacrifice. When she returned to the Soviet Union in 1939 she left the ms at the University of Basel. It has been suggested that she was persuaded by accounts of her husband, Sergei Efron's experiences in the White Army (which he found very different from the legendary heroes she describes) not to publish it. This is not so: only an accident, namely a quarrel with the Paris editors of Latest News, prevented the poems appearing there in 1928. Ironically, the quarrel arose out of Tsvetaeva's admiration for poetry written in the Soviet Union.

p. 49 Ry-azan: the voice names a town near Moscow, and Tsvetaeva breaks the word, drawing out the long syllable to mime the accent of peasants who live there.

On a Red Horse

p. 54 This poem was written in five days in January 1921 .

God help us   Smoke!

p. 63 Written on 30 September 1922, shortly after Tsvetaeva and her daughter Alya joined Efron in Czechoslovakia.

necklace of coins: the note on p. 748 of the Moscow-Leningrad edition suggests the reference is to a doorman or hall-porter wearing many medals.

Ophelia: In Defence of the Queen

p. 64   One of a run of epistolary poems; there is another written as if from Ophelia to Hamlet on the same date (28 February 1923).

Wires

p. 65   A note on p. 749 of the 1965 edition says: 'from a cycle of 10 poems… inspired by the correspondence with Pasternak which began in June 1922, soon after Tsvetaeva went abroad, and which continued for many years. Under Tsvetaeva's draft of no. 4 there is a note which later went into a letter to Pasternak: "Poems are the tracks by which I enter your soul. But your soul recedes and I get impatient, I jump ahead, blindly on the off chance, and then I wait in trepidation: will it turn my way?"…'

p. 65   Poem 1: rigging: a number of puns in the Russian original make this a less conventional image than it might appear. 'Atlantic', for example, is contrasted with 'Pacific' meaning tranquil.

distance: again much word-play is lost in translation: 'receding' contains a syllable '*dal*' meaning distance, and '*zhal*' (pity) picks this up as a rhyme.

still implored: the Russian makes clear that it is the distance that is being implored by the voices.

p. 68   Poem 4: The Leila of your lips: this is puzzling. Tatiana Retivov suggests a reference to Bizet's heroine Leila in *The Pearl Fishers*, with whom several characters in the opera fall in love.

p. 70   Poem 8: The white book of the distant River Don: Tsvetaeva is contrasting the black books of sorcery with her passionate reading about the fate of the White Army, who made an important stand on the River Don.

Sahara

p. 73   This poem is written at the height of Tsvetaeva's passionate correspondence with the twenty-year-old critic, Alexander Bakhrakh, whom she had never met, but upon whose loving support she depended so strongly that a break in his flow of letters brought her almost to collapse.

Poem of the Mountain

p. 86   After helping to settle her daughter Alya in a boarding-school in Moravia during August 1923, Tsvetaeva took a flat alone on the wooded hill at the centre of Prague. During the autumn of 1923 she had the most passionate love affair of her life with Konstantin Borisovich Rodzevitch, regarded by the émigrés of Prague as a White officer, though he had in fact fought with the Red Navy.

p. 89   Hagar: Abraham's slave and concubine, who bore him a son, Ishmael, was sent away at the insistence of Abraham's wife Sarah and went to live in the Arabian desert.

p. 90   twelve apostles: Tsvetaeva is probably referring to the clock tower on the Old Town Square in Prague, where the twelve apostles appear as the hour strikes.

Poem of the End

p. 94   There are fourteen poems in this cycle (some divided into two or three lyrics); the eleventh poem is not translated.

The love affair with Rodzevitch was over by December 1923, and this poem records exactly how she learns of his decision to end their relationship, as they meet, walk about the city of Prague with its many bridges, and talk over café tables.

p. 96   a window under the roof.../it is burning?: a rephrasing of lines from a poem by Blok.

who shall I tell my sorrow: words from the Psalter.

p. 96   Semiramis: Assyrian princess (c.800 BC) famous for her hanging gardens, one of the Seven Wonders of the World.

p. 98   Star of Malta: the emblem of a medieval knightly order.

p. 98   powder/made by Berthold Schwartz: gunpowder.

p. 101   The stamp left on your heart/would be the ring on your hand: an allusion to the Song of Songs (8:6): 'Set me as a seal upon thine heart...'

p. 110   Khlebnikov: a Russian Futurist poet.

p. 115   Marinkas: Marinka is a diminutive of Marina, a common Polish name (and well-known to Russians from the princess in Pushkin's *Boris Godunov*).

New Year's Greetings

p. 121   Ariadna Efron writes that the correspondence between Tsvetaeva and Pasternak began in 1922, and continued until 1935. It was at its most intense in the mid-1920s. The correspondence between Tsvetaeva and Rilke was set in motion by a letter from Leonid Pasternak written to congratulate Rilke on his fiftieth birthday. Rilke, then in a sanitorium with leukaemia, replied warmly, mentioning that the fame of Leonid's son Boris had reached him from all sides, and praising particularly poems which had been translated into French by Helene Izvolskaya and published in Paul Valéry's journal *Commerce*. Boris had to wait for his father to send him a copy of Rilke's letter, which was too precious to be risked in the post. In his first letter to Rilke Pasternak asked the poet he so admired to send a copy of *Duino Elegies* to Marina

Tsvetaeva, whom he described as ' a born poet, a great talent...' More practically, he asked Rilke to send any reply through Tsvetaeva, since there was no direct post between the USSR and Switzerland. The first exchanges between Tsvetaeva and Rilke were ecstatic on both sides. But Tsvetaeva longed for greater intimacy and even a meeting, unaware that Rilke was already in the final months of his life. She was wounded by his subsequent silence. Her elegy for Rilke was written in the days following his death.

p. 122   German is as native to me as Russian: Tsvetaeva had been brought up by her mother to speak and read German fluently.

p. 124   Baobab: a strange tropical tree native to Africa which looks as if its branches were roots. Many creatures live in the branches. The Baobab has gathered many superstitions around it.

The Ratcatcher

p. 125   These are three sections from a long narrative poem which follows the story of the Pied Piper. It is marked throughout with a disgust for material well-being, so that the abundance in the town is felt as a direct cause of the plague of rats. In later sections of the poem the burghers give the flute-player a contemptuous dressing-down on the use of his art. D.S. Mirsky wrote of 'The Ratcatcher': '... it is not only a verbal structure that is astounding in its richness and harmony, it is also a serious "political"... and "ethical" satire.' Tsvetaeva began writing the poem in Vshenory in early 1925, and completed it in Paris in November that year.

p. 128   poods: a Russian measure.

Poems to a Son

p. 132   Georgy returned to Russia with Tsvetaeva in 1939, to join his father and sister. When they were arrested he lived with his mother until they were evacuated to Yelabuga. After Tsvetaeva died, he left to join the army and died, still in his teens, in the defence of Moscow.

Homesickness

p. 133   Kamchatka: a far-eastern Siberian peninsula, sometimes invoked in the sense of 'back of beyond'.

Epitaph

p. 136   These poems were written for N.P. Gronsky, a young poet killed in a street accident when he was twenty-four. Tsvetaeva had been close to him as a young boy of eighteen in Meudon, and continued to value his poetry highly after they stopped seeing one another.

Desk

p. 141　Three lyrics from a sequence of six.

p. 142　thirty years: the lyrics were written between 1933 and 1935, and Tsvetaeva must have had in mind her very earliest attempts at poetry.

Bus

p. 145　Easter toys: on Palm Sunday most Russian towns held markets at which sweets, trinkets, and small devils and cherubim were commonly sold.

p. 146　A moist, wood-twig smoke of green: although this verse appears to be another draft of the previous one, both appear in the Moscow-Leningrad edition.

p. 147　Nebuchadnezzar: cf. Daniel, 4:31–3.

p. 150　thief: there is multiple punning on the idea of pillaging as a form of (literal) 'ripping-off', or fleecing, throughout the passage.

Poems to Czechoslovakia

p. 153　Tsvetaeva was thinking of the region known to her as 'Chekhia' in the country we have until recently called Czechoslovakia.

Vary/Tatras: Karlovy vary (Karlsbad), a famous spa in western Czechoslovakia. By mentioning it along with 'Tatry', the Tatras, mountain ranges in the eastern part of that country, Tsvetaeva means to emphasise that the Germans took the whole of the country, and all the pleasures that it offered.

they won: 'won' in Russian can also mean 'took'.

spittle: the original poem is headed by a sentence from the newspapers of March 1939: 'The Czechs went up to the Germans and spat.'

p. 154　give back to God his ticket: this is a reference to Ivan Karamazov (in Dostoyevsky's *Brothers Karamazov*), who defiantly offered back to God his entrance ticket to Heaven so long as Heaven is built upon or despite the suffering of children on earth.

Select Bibliography of Works in English

Joseph Brodsky, *Less than One: Selected Essays* (New York, Farrar, Straus, and Giroux 1986)

Lily Feiler, *Marina Tsvetaeva: The Double Beat of Heaven and Hell* (Durham NC and London, Duke University Press 1994)

Elaine Feinstein, *A Captive Lion: The Life of Marina Tsvetaeva* (London, Hutchinson 1987)

Elaine Feinstein (trans.), *Selected Poems of Marina Tsvetaeva* (Oxford University Press 1971; paperback enlarged edition, Oxford University Press 1981; third edition re-issued Hutchinson 1986; fourth, further enlarged, edition, with revised introduction, Oxford Poets, Oxford University Press 1993; enlarged fifth edition Carcanet Press 1999)

Simon Karlinsky, *Marina Tsvetaeva: The Woman, Her World and Her Poetry* (Cambridge, Cambridge University Press 1985)

Robin Kemball (trans.), Marina Tsvetaeva, *The Demesne of the Swans: a bi-lingual edition* (Ann Arbor, Ardis 1980)

J. Marin King (ed.), *A Captive Spirit: Selected Prose of Marina Tsvetayeva* (Ann Arbor, Ardis 1980)

Nina Kossman (trans.), *Poem of the End: Selected Lyrical and Narrative Poetry by Marina Tsvetaeva, with facing Russian text* (Ann Arbor, Ardis 1995)

Irma Kudrova, *Death of a Poet: The Last Days of Marina Tsvetaeva*, trans. Mary Ann Szporluk (London, Duckworth 2004)

Angela Livingstone (trans.) *Art in the Light of Conscience: Eight Essays on Poetry by Marina Tsvetaeva* (London, Bristol Classical 1992)

Angela Livingstone (trans.), Marina Tsvetaeva, *The Ratcatcher: A Lyrical Satire* (London, Angel Press 1999)

David McDuff (trans.), Marina Tsvetaeva, *Selected Poems* (Newcastle, Bloodaxe 1987)

Boris Pasternak, *An Essay in Autobiography*, trans. Manya Harari (London, Collins and Harvill Press 1959)

Yevgeny Pasternak, Yelena Pasternak and Konstantin M. Azadovsky (eds), *Boris Pasternak, Marina Tsvetayeva, Rainer Maria Rilke: Letters, Summer 1926*, trans. Margaret Wettlin and Walter

Arndt (London, Jonathan Cape 1986)

Ellendea Proffer, *Tsvetaeva: A Pictorial Biography*, trans. J. Marin King (Ann Arbor, Ardis 1980)

Viktoria Schweitzer, *Tsvetaeva*, trans. Robert Chandler and H.T. Willetts (London, HarperCollins 1992)

Jane A. Taubman, A *Life Through Poetry: Marina Tsvetaeva's Lyric Diary* (Columbus, OH, Slavica Publishers 1989)

Appendix

Note to 1971 edition: On Working Method

No poet's voice can be exactly recorded in the medium of another language. Marina Tsvetaeva's is particularly difficult to capture, both because her consistent adherence to rhyme and to metrical regularity would, if copied in the English poems, probably enfeeble them, and because so many of the linguistic devices which she powerfully exploits (such as ellipsis, changes of word-order, the throwing into relief of inflectional endings) are simply not available in English. On the whole, the English versions are consciously less emphatic, less loudly-spoken, less violent, often less jolting and disturbing than the Russian originals. Most noticeable of all in Tsvetaeva's poems, especially the later ones, are the very strong rhythm and the unprecedently vigorous syntax. There is, too, a somewhat idiosyncratic and highly emotional use of punctuation, particularly of exclamation marks and dashes.

Except in the case of the 'Poem of the Mountain', a literal version of which was prepared by Valentina Coe, and a number of earlier poems, where the literal version was dictated on to a tape-recorder, Elaine Feinstein and I worked as follows: I would write out each poem in English, keeping as close as made sense to the word-order of the Russian; joining by hyphens those English words which represented a single Russian word; indicating by oblique lines words whose order had to be reversed to be readable, and by asterisks phrases where several changes had had to take place; adding notes on metre, sound properties, play with word-roots, and specifically Russian connotations. All this *material* was then changed into poetry by Elaine Feinstein, who took those liberties with it that the new English poem demanded, but returned constantly to the Russian text to check the look, sound, and position of Tsvetaeva's own words.

To give one example – the opening of lyric 6 of 'Poem of the End'. One of the most original and effective features of the poems making up this cycle is the way they tend to be structurally based each upon a single syntactic unit which is several times repeated almost identically. This determines the structure of every stanza in which it appears, throwing into different kinds of relief the words and phrases that are not part of it, and bringing a peculiar rhythm into the expressed emotions. When it ceases to recur, we read the rest of the poem in strong recollection of its shape.

In lyric 6 the dominant phrase (*italicised*, by me, in the extract below) is one that has the verb 'to hand' as its final and basic element, and involves the prominent use of the dative case. Each time, the phrase is in brackets and, each time, its last word comes as an enjambment. It occurs in stanzas 2, 3 and 5; is implied in stanza 4; and is referred to (through similar enjambment and rhythm) in stanza 6, where a sharp irony arises from the combination of the rhythm and pattern of that unit with the idea of 'dividing' – the opposite, one would think, of 'handing'. Here are those six stanzas, in Russian and 'literal' English. (I omit my notes on diction, connotations, etc.)

2

…

(Da, v chas, kogda poyezd podan,	(Yes, at the-hour when the-train is-served,
Vy zhenshchinam, kak bokal,	*You to-women, like a-goblet,*
pechal'nuyu chest' ukhoda	*The-sorrowful honour of-departure*

3

Vruchayete…) – Mozhet, bred?	*Hand…) –* Perhaps, delirium?
Oslyshalsa? (Lzhets uchtiviy,	I-misheard? (Courteous liar,
Lyubovnitse kak buket	*To-you-lover like a-bouquet*
Krovavuyu chest' razryva	*The-bloody honour of-rift*

4

Vruchayushchi…) – Vnyatno: slog	*Handing…)* (It's)-clear: syllable
Za slogom, itak – prostimsa,	After syllable, so – let's-say-goodbye,
Skazalivy? (Kakplatok	You/said? (*Like a-handkerchief*
V chas sladostnovo beschinstva	*At the-hour of-voluptuous recklessness*

5

Uronenny...) – Bitvy sei	*Dropped...) – Of-this/battle*
Vy – Tsezar'. (O, vypad nagly!	*You-are Caesar. (O, insolent/*
	thrust!
Protivniku – kak trofei,	*To-(your)-opponent – like a trophy,*
Im otdannuyu zhe shpagu	*The very sabre that he surrendered*

6

Vruchat'!) – Prodolzhayet. (Zvon	*To-hand!) – It-continues. (Sound*
V ushakh...) – Preklonyayus'	*In (my)-ears...) I-bow twice:*
dvazhdy:	
Vpervye operezhon	For-the-first-time-I-am-forestalled
Vrazryve. – Vy eto kazhdoi?	In a-rift. – Do-you-(say) this to-
	every-(woman)?

7

Ne oprovergaite! Mest'	Don't deny-(it)! A-vengeance
Dostoinaya Lovelasa.	Worthy of-Lovelace.
Zhest, delayushchi vam chest',	*A-gesture doing you honour,*
A ne rzvodyashchi myaso	*But for-me dividing the-flesh*

8

Ot kosti.	*From the-bone.*

All subsequent instances of the dative case in this poem stand out strongly because of this established pattern: as, for example, the 'Do you say this to everyone?' in stanza 6; the later plea not to speak of their love to anyone coming after; and, especially, the final interchange about whether to give each other a parting gift such as a ring or a book.

Different syntactic patterns dominate other lyrics in the cycle. Their presence, as a fundamental structure, is typical of the whole of 'Poem of the End', and is a device which Tsvetaeva has elaborated with complete originality.

Angela Livingstone